ESSENTIAL PSYCHOLOGY

General Editor
Peter Herriot

B1

SOCIAL BEHAVIOUR

D0522337

ESSENTIAL

PSYCHOLOGY

SOCIAL
BEHAVIOUR

Key problems and social relevance

Kevin Wheldall

Methuen

First published in 1975 by Methuen & Co Ltd
11 New Fetter Lane, London EC4P 4EE
© 1975 Kevin Wheldall
Printed in Great Britain by
Richard Clay (The Chaucer Press), Ltd
Bungay, Suffolk
ISBN (hardback) 416 82010 7
ISBN (paperback) 416 82020 4

Contents

Preface

This is *not* a textbook in social psychology if by textbook we mean an exhaustive overview of the entire field of social psychology reviewing alternative theoretical perspectives. It is an introduction, just that. My primary aim is to encourage someone who has ventured an interest in social psychology into pursuing that interest a little further. I believe social psychology can be fascinating; I want others to discover this for themselves. As such, this book is not for existing social psychologists – they are, or should be, convinced of its value already.

The material I have selected and the approach I have taken are more a reflection of me than of social psychology as it stands. If you dislike the book, blame me, not social psychology. The approach I have taken will not necessarily be reflected in the succeeding books in this unit of the series: they too will reflect the interests and personalities of their authors. I have attempted to introduce the methods and the sort of topics social psychologists are interested in. Some topics are merely touched upon because a more thorough exposition is provided in other texts within the series but others are covered in more detail on the grounds of my personal interest, or relevance, or because they will not be included in other texts.

Perhaps I should make a special point about the behavioural orientation I have adopted. I believe that learning theory is and will be an increasingly important consideration within social psychology. Many social psychologists will disagree with me

7

but I want the newcomer to the science at least to have the option of encountering learning theory – an option which was effectively closed to me until after graduation and an approach which is ignored in many introductory texts. I have not attempted to explain all the phenomena discussed in behavioural terms – I could not – and anyway I have sympathy with Roger Brown who states that, 'it is not a service to social psychology to pretend that a trivial verbal integration is the same thing as a genuine theoretical integration'.

As I have said, this book is a reflection of me; I believe that social psychology can be both fun and relevant. Social psychology is the nearest we have got to a scientific understanding of social phenomena. It provides a framework for analysing societal problems which we may attempt to remedy by applying the scientifically established principles of learning.

Although the responsibility for this book is totally mine I would like to acknowledge the help and advice I've received from friends and colleagues; Roslyn Hope who scrutinized my scribbled manuscript and made many helpful suggestions; Kathleen Pitt who deciphered it, diplomatically 'adjusted' my spelling and typed beautiful drafts; Peter Herriot, mentor and friend, who provided reassurance and ideas; Peter Mittler, my supervisor, without whose patient coaching my style would have been even worse; Tony, John, Caro and Dorrie, my London friends, who gave the non-psychologist's opinion and provided anecdotes, quotes, warmth, humour and understanding. I would also like to thank my parents for their continual interest and support.

Editor's Introduction

Many psychologists feel that social psychology has been relatively neglected in the past. A major objective of psychology is to shed light on why people behave as they do in 'real life'; since a large proportion of our waking lives is spent in relating to other people, it follows that psychology should devote considerable attention to understanding social behaviour. Kevin Wheldall points out how individuals' behaviour can be described in terms of social influences acting upon them. Social psychology, in other words, provides a theoretical framework within which to analyse behaviour. The social psychologist's study can range from actual face-to-face situations to the effects of a person's general cultural environment on his behaviour. He can also reverse the picture, and observe how an individual can act upon his social environment in such a way as to change it. Kevin Wheldall selects a few of the key topics in social psychology, and explores them from a theoretical and practical point of view. Theoretically he applies the concepts of behaviourism; practically, he shows how society might change if account were taken of some of the findings of social psychology.

Social Behaviour belongs to Unit B of *Essential Psychology*. What unifies the books in this unit is their subject matter; all deal with the individual in society. In order to cope adequately with their findings, social psychologists have had to develop different conceptual frameworks. The analogy of a human being as a computer (employed in Unit A) may be appropriate, perhaps, to some one-to-one interpersonal situations. But to do justice to what happens in groups, new concepts (e.g. role) and new models (e.g. dynamic models) have been more useful. The reader will find other general conceptual frameworks in other units. They are not so much mutually contradictory as efforts to do justice to the complexities of psychology's subject matter. Living with a variety of explanatory frameworks decreases our confidence in psychology as a mature science; but perhaps it is better to be honest about what we don't know.

Essential Psychology as a whole is designed to reflect the changing structure and function of psychology. The authors are both academic and professionals, and their aim has been to introduce the most important concepts in their areas to be-ginning students. They have tried to do so clearly but have not attempted to conceal the fact that concepts that now appear central to their work may soon be peripheral. In other words, they have presented psychology as a developing set of views of man, not as a body of received truth. Readers are not intended to study the whole series in order to 'master the basics'. Rather, since different people may wish to use different theoretical frameworks for their own purposes, the series has been designed so that each title stands on its own. But it is possible that if the reader has read no psychology before, he will enjoy individual books more if he has read the introductions (A1, B1, etc.) to the units to which they belong. Readers of the units concerned with applications of psychology (E, F) may benefit from reading all the introductions.

A word about references in the text to the work of other writers – e.g. 'Smith, 1974'. These occur where the author feels he must acknowledge (by name) an important concept or some crucial evidence. The book or article referred to will be listed in the references (which double as name index) at the back of the book. The reader is invited to consult these sources if he wishes to explore topics further. A list of general further reading is also to be found at the back of this book.

We hope you enjoy psychology.

Peter Herriot

I
Introduction

A car skids to a halt a few yards past me on the motorway approach. 'Hop in mate, I can take you as far as Northampton.' I settle myself among cartons and display boards advertising a new brand of cat food.

'We've got a big promotion on,' he offers in explanation. 'I'm a rep. What are you? ... a student?'

'Well research, actually,' I mutter. 'And I lecture as well.'

'I see.... What are you studying then?'

This is the question I've been dreading; my answer to this question activates a totally predictable sequence. Shall I try and bluff it out with 'Taxidermy' or 'Brewing Sciences'?

'Psychology,' I whisper quickly, trying to look engrossed in a field of cows.

'Psychology, really? Well, it's funny you should say that 'cos I'm a bit of a psychologist myself.'

I smile politely, teeth clenched.

'Oh yes,' he continues. 'Can always tell what a person's like by just looking at him. Take you for instance; I'm not a bit surprised that you're a student psychiatrist. Don't start trying to psycho-analyse me now!'

I moan softly and wonder where to start or whether to bother.

'No, no, I'm a lecturer in psychology,' I begin hesitantly. 'Not psychiatry – I'm concerned with why people behave the way they do in everyday social life. I'm a social psychologist,' I finish flatly.

'What's that, then?' he asks suspiciously.

11

'A psychologist who likes parties perhaps . . .' I volunteer.

He smiles and asks what social psychology is really all about. What do social psychologists do? And why? And how do they set about it?

And these are precisely the questions you, the newcomer to social psychology, are likely to ask. You probably already have an idea what psychology is; and also know that psychiatry is a branch of medical science concerned with the treatment of mental illness. Psychology's scope is much broader, encompassing the study of the behaviour of both man and animals. Psychology has been called the science of mental life, the study of mind, the scientific study of behaviour – and many more things, some less than flattering.

Various, more precise definitions have been attempted:

An academic discipline, a profession, and a science dealing with the study of mental processes and behaviour in man and animals. Not to be confused with the medical speciality of psychiatry.
(*A Psychiatric Glossary,* 1964)

A branch of science dealing with *behaviour, acts,* or *mental processes,* and with the *mind, self* or *person* who behaves, acts or has the mental processes. . . . (*English and English,* 1958)

The main point I want to emphasize is that psychology is a *science.* Its roots, as we shall see, lie in philosopy but today it espouses the scientific method and proceeds by means of careful, detailed experimentation. To kill another myth, it is not an occult science. Its main areas of study are not mind-reading, fortune-telling or phrenology. You are unlikely to see many party tricks in a psychological laboratory but some psychologists do carry out scientific research into 'para-normal phenomena' such as extra-sensory perception (E.S.P.) and hypnotic states. The second point that I would emphasize is that psychology has become a science of *behaviour.* Armchair philosophizing and introspective speculation and conjecture have given way to a concern with the facts of what animals, including man, do. Before we consider the history of psychology, and in particular social psychology, any further, however, we ought to attempt to define what social psychology is and what distinguishes it from psychology in general.

Sprott (1952) attempts to define social psychology in the following way:

Social psychology is concerned with the ways in which a person's conduct and dispositions are influenced by the conducts and dispositions of other people.

Unfortunately, this does not tell us nearly enough. Eysenck and Arnold (1972) attempt a more detailed answer by listing the areas of study of interest to social psychologists.

The study of the following topics tends to be identified with social psychology: social influences on abilities and behaviour, attitudes, social norms, group dynamics, communication, role and status, leadership, conflict and cooperation, inter-group relations, crime and delinquency, authoritarianism and machiavellianism, belief systems and value orientations, socialization, person perception, social learning and conformity.

This is a very thorough listing but in order to understand many of the terms you need to be a social psychologist already! As we can see, social psychology is very difficult to define. Brown (1965), in possibly the best, if now slightly dated, introduction to social psychology available, recognizes this.

Social psychology is a net of topics that have exceeded the grasp of a non-social psychology but which are being effectively investigated by a psychology that draws upon the social sciences. ... I myself cannot find any single attribute or any combination of attributes that will clearly distinguish the topics of social psychology from topics that remain within general experimental psychology, or sociology or anthropology or linguistics.... Social psychology is concerned with the mental processes (or behaviour) of persons insofar as these are determined by past or present inter-action with other persons, but this is rough and it is not a definition that excludes very much.... [Social psychology] is a field of study, an historical development, not a theoretical construct.

From this we can see that the boundaries of social psychology are difficult to define, especially where social psychology borders with sociology. A rough distinction would be to say that sociologists are usually concerned with larger units of society than social psychologists. A sociologist might be interested in the family as a unit, a social psychologist would be more likely to be interested in the influence of the family on an individual member or members. But, as McGrath (1970) says:

13

Social psychology can be viewed as a sub-field within psychology or sociology or as a linking interdisciplinary field of study analogous to the field of biophysics.

McGrath goes on to argue that social psychology may be said to be concerned with studying social phenomena at three levels – 'the individual, the small groups of which he is a part and the total society and culture within which he is embedded'.

Perhaps the reader can now appreciate my hitch-hiking dilemma, for even now we have not arrived at a satisfactory statement of what social psychology is about. We do have a rough idea, however, of the sort of topics in which the social psychologist is interested and as we proceed to explore some of these areas we will see more clearly the approaches and methods which characterize social psychology.

A brief historical perspective

If social psychology is so difficult to define and distinguish from other approaches, how did it ever develop as a separate entity? As Brown (1965) says, social psychology is a 'historical development' and to answer this question we must take a brief look into social psychology's past.

The most important thing to note is how recent a science social psychology is. Although its roots stretch back to the social philosophers of ancient Greece such as Plato and Aristotle, it has only really come into being in this century. Zajonc claimed in 1966 that 'more than 90% of all social psychological research has been carried out during the last twenty years and most of it during the last ten'. The first social psychological experiment as such was not carried out until 1897 by Triplett. His simple experiment consisted of measuring how long a person took to complete 130 winds on a fishing-rod reel when carrying out the task alone and comparing it with the performance of the person when competing against another. He found that the effect of competition was to improve performance, i.e. subjects wound quicker when competing against each other.

Theories of social behaviour were being proposed thousands of years before the first experiment, however. As already noted, Plato and Aristotle both wrote about the organization and struc-

14

ture of society. In *The Republic*, Plato outlined his ideas for the formation of an ideal society. Many hundreds of years later, the British seventeenth- and eighteenth-century philosophers were speculating on the nature of man and the forces influencing his actions. They tended to put forward single-factor, uni-causal theories of social behaviour. Thomas Hobbes favoured the notion of power; Adam Smith preferred self-interest; whereas Jeremy Bentham, building on earlier hedonistic ideas, put forward the 'pleasure principle'. None of these philosophical theories, however, amounted to more than mere speculation; none of them was investigated scientifically.

Theories of social behaviour were also put forward by the early sociologists. Auguste Comte, the founding father of sociology, attempted to solve the problem of how man could change society and also be changed by it at the same time. Later theorists such as LeBon, attempting to account for this, put forward the notion of a 'group mind' which limited individual autonomy, coupled with the idea of imitation by which man was influenced by fellow members of society. Imitation, as a means of learning, is now accepted within psychology but again it must be stressed that it has now been scientifically investigated and shown to be effective. Imitation does not work, as LeBon speculated, through a 'group mind'.

Emile Durkheim emphasized the empirical approach to sociology. He argued against speculation in favour of facts. In his famous study of the phenomenon of suicide he combined statistical data relating to political, religious and family life to determine the variables which were predictive of suicide. He found, for example, that single persons were more likely to commit suicide than married persons.

The rise of social psychology was also influenced by early clinical or abnormal psychology. The work of Charcot on hypnosis and, more importantly, Freud's theories of the unconscious self, led to a concern with the irrational, uncontrollable, unconscious forces which were said to affect man's behaviour. Freudian concepts were popular topics of investigation by social psychologists, but today Freudian psychology is much less influential.

Before stressing the influence of general, experimental psychology we should note the contribution of Darwin and of anthropologists such as Boas, Margaret Mead and Ruth Benedict.

Darwin's theory of evolution was of considerable importance in altering the prevalent mode of thought of the day, influencing, among others, Karl Marx who was impressed by his emphasis on the struggle for survival. Darwin placed great stress on the notion of competition as an evolutionary force but what is not often remembered is his insistence that cooperation and inter-dependence have considerable survival value for a species.

The early anthropologists served as a timely restraint on those who would generalize about human behaviour. They pointed to the diversity of systems for organizing social be-haviour and also to the many and various 'human natures'. Their cross-cultural approach showed that much that was taken for granted as innate or universal or common sense was not the case and that human social behaviour varied enormously.

The early experimental psychologists demonstrated that the traditional methods of science were equally applicable to psy-chology. They showed that it was possible to study human be-haviour by means of laboratory experiments in the tradition of the physical sciences. The influence of this on social psychology was to create a sub-field of experimental social psychology, an approach which is very prominent in modern social psychology.

The first books on social psychology both appeared in 1908; McDougall, a British psychologist, provided an *Introduction to Social Psychology*, and Ross, an American sociolo-gist, produced *Social Psychology*. McDougall's theory of in-stincts will be discussed more fully in Chapter 4 but we should note at this point the heavy emphasis he put on the innate de-terminants of social behaviour. The first real social psychology book, however (by which I mean a book based on the results of experiments), was published by Allport in 1924, again called *Social Psychology*. Whilst agreeing with McDougall's concern with the individual, he rejected his instinctual theories in favour of a view of social behaviour as being influenced by learning in line with the newly emerging *behaviourist* school of psychology. Allport extended the concept of conditioned reflexes (discussed later) to account for social phenomena such as emotional ex-perience, crowd behaviour, language development, suggestion, imitation and social facilitation.

Behaviourism, pioneered by Watson, was characterized by extreme objectivity. Heavily influenced by the Russian physi-

16

ologist, Pavlov, Watson demanded that concepts be both carefully defined and experimentally demonstrable. Freudian notions and instinctual theories were rejected on both of these grounds; they were vague and virtually untestable. Alternative explanations of behaviour were offered in terms of conditioning paradigms which we will discuss in detail later in the following chapter. Watson was so convinced of the importance of learning rather than unproven innate behaviour that he once made the following statement:

Give me a dozen healthy infants, well formed, and my own specified world to bring them up in and I'll guarantee to take any one at random and train him to become any type of specialist I might select – doctor, lawyer, artist, merchant-chief and, yes, even beggar-man and thief, regardless of his talents, penchants, tendencies, abilities, vocation and race of his ancestors.

This is extreme environmentalism – the belief that human behaviour is totally learned from the environment in which the person is reared. It is directly opposed to nativism, the belief that a person's potential is biologically fixed at birth. This latter view would see personality and intelligence as being determined by genetic factors. Both Freudian and instinctual theory are basically nativistic.

The nature/nurture controversy has been of central importance in psychology's development and has recently re-surfaced in the heated arguments over race and I.Q. which have spilled over into the non-academic press. To put the 'story so far' in a nutshell, we might say that the nativist position held sway until the rise of behaviourism in the 1920s. Early behaviourism itself, however, soon also met considerable criticism, generated at least in part by Watson's extremism and the lack of adequate theoretical paradigms. Some of the theories of learning proposed were barely more credible than instinct theory and were generalized to cover more complex behaviour without adequate foundation. Today, behaviourism is becoming acceptable again, largely through the work of B. F. Skinner and his followers. Behaviour modification, the applied use of operant conditioning techniques to enable people such as the mentally ill and handicapped to learn new, more appropriate behaviour, has been shown to work effectively and efficiently. This has convinced most psychologists that animals, including man, *can* learn in this way, whilst

17

many would go further and say that man learns only in this way.

This brief survey of social psychology's history has reviewed the influences on the formation of what we today recognize as the science of social psychology. We have credited Allport's *Social Psychology* as marking the start of 'real' social psychology, but what has happened since then? To answer this question now would negate the need for the rest of the book. The more recent major influences on social psychology will be credited in the various chapters on what I see as being the major areas of interest. Present-day social psychology is expanding considerably and is becoming increasingly concerned with itself: its methodology; the ethics of social research and the relevance of social psychology – all of which will be discussed later in this chapter.

The relevance of social psychology

Social psychology can be far from boring and can help us to understand social problems with increasing insight into their causation. This is not to say that it all makes gripping reading or that it is all relevant to everyday life. Indeed, some social psychologists seem to go out of their way to make their subject as dull as possible, haunted perhaps by a need to ape the 'respectable' physical sciences. All too often, concepts that most people could understand are hidden behind a cloak of jargon.

Similarly, it is sometimes difficult to understand why social psychologists ever embarked on certain areas of study. The topics themselves seem so trivial, if not irrelevant, and often they are approached so ploddingly that any spark of life is stamped out. It seems especially sad that scientists given the fascinating scope of social psychology should pick topics and approaches characterized by irrelevance, heavy-handedness and yawn-inspiring boredom. Happily, however, there is much in social psychology which is prone to none of these ailments. A recent collection of readings edited by Swingle (1973) provides a wealth of studies geared to demonstrating *Social Psychology in Everyday Life*. Swingle declares himself to be unhappy with the traditional reply to the question: 'What does social psychology have to do with real life?', which he summarizes as follows:

Experimental social psychology has been and still is, largely a laboratory-based operation, because in the laboratory researchers can isolate variables of interest for close and highly controlled observation. The regularities thus observed then contribute to the development of social psychological theory, which (if it is a good theory) should be applicable to natural social settings.

As he rightly says, however, the laboratory-based approach, for all its rigour, may yield results which do not hold in the everyday world. The studies he selects are characterized (a) by their scientific approach and (b) by their immediate relevance to everyday life, which is achieved by carrying out the experiments in the everyday world.

One of the most interesting studies he includes is engagingly entitled *Bumper Stickers and the Cops* (Heussenstamm, 1971). This study investigates unfair discrimination against Black Panther Party supporters by the police. Members of the party had complained that they had received so many traffic citations that they were in danger of losing their licences. It was noted that they all had party affiliation badges or stickers glued to the bumpers of their cars. In order to put their grievance to the test, fifteen drivers who had no record of traffic offences for the previous year attached Black Panther Party stickers to their cars. The fifteen drivers consisted of a mixed group of male and female students of black, white and Mexican descent, all of whom promised to drive according to the law. The appearance of the drivers varied from short-haired 'straights' to long-haired 'freaks'. The cars, which varied from hippie vans to standard American makes, were all checked for defective equipment (lights, brakes etc.). The only thing the cars had in common was a lurid day-glo orange and black 'Black Panther' sticker attached to the rear bumper.

The results were immediate and alarming. The first traffic violation ticket was received by a student within two hours of the start of the study, five other tickets were received by students the next day and so it went on until thirty-three citations had been received in seventeen days. Some of the students had to withdraw from the study within a week as they had already received three tickets each and the receipt of a fourth could have resulted in their losing their driving licences. Tickets were received regardless of race or sex or appearance.

As it is unlikely that previously safe drivers would suddenly all start driving badly, it is reasonable to assume that the evidence indicates bias by the police against drivers sporting 'Black Panther' stickers. This is a striking example of social psychology in a real life situation where a simple experiment demonstrated what the Panthers had already suspected.

But if it was 'common sense' in that the Panthers already suspected it, why bother doing the experiment? This is a common criticism of psychology generally. People either say 'I can't see the point of investigating that' or 'I could have told you that before you started'. Unfortunately 'common sense' is not very reliable and is often contradictory. As Lindgren (1969) says, ' "Common sense" usually refers to a body of information derived from mature experience and carries implications of hardheadedness and objectivity. The term can, however, be used by anyone or any group to justify a wide range of actions, some of them quite irrational.'

Proverbs are good examples of common sense. You experience misfortune and someone tells you 'every cloud has a silver lining'; then you meet the pessimist next door who remarks that 'it never rains but it pours'. Unless you are superstitious, neither of these sayings is psychologically predictive anyway, but take the case of being parted from a loved one. You may be told 'absence makes the heart grow fonder', or 'out of sight, out of mind'. Both may be true, the former operating initially but giving way to the latter over time. A psychological approach would be to test this out empirically, varying the time intervals. Our results would more likely point to individual variability, however, supporting possibly the most apt saying of all, that 'there's nowt so queer as folk'! Psychologists often set out to test commonsense predictions but although common sense or popular belief are occasionally validated, often they are not as we shall see during the course of this book.

The methods of social psychology (see A8)

The methods of research in social psychology are many and various. The basis, as in all sciences, is the scientific method but social psychology has also necessitated the building up of an idiosyncratic methodology to cope with the sort of problems in which social psychologists are interested. It would be impossible and undesirable to give both a grounding in general scientific method and survey the more specific social psychological research techniques in an introductory book such as this but there are some general points which we will need to bear in mind to understand the experiments reported in this book. In addition we will consider a few examples of the difficulties social psychologists come up against and how they set about solving them.

The scientific approach is often said to require no metaphysical propositions. This is not always strictly true, because in believing that an experiment repeated under identical physical conditions will always yield the same results, the scientist is assuming that the Laws of Causality (that every event has a cause) will always hold. But as David Hume (1711–76) pointed out, the proposition that the laws of causality will operate in the future is unverifiable. Thus the scientist must make an act of faith about causality and his approach is sensu stricto metaphysical. Nevertheless, a distinction can be made between the scientific approach, in which every assumption, except that of causality is open to empirical verification and the metaphysical approach, which may involve many unverifiable assumptions.

(McFarland and McFarland, 1969)

If this is the scientific method which is the basis for the science of social psychology, how do we go about establishing the causes of social behaviour? Basically, we are concerned with collecting data to test hypotheses about social behaviour. We can collect the necessary data in two main ways, by means of *experimental methods* or *non-experimental/observational methods*. Both approaches have advantages and disadvantages. The experimental method quite simply requires a controlled experiment to be carried out. The experiment in its simplest form will concentrate on establishing the factors which cause or otherwise influence a certain behaviour. The means by which we choose to measure the certain behaviour is known as the *dependent variable*. Hence, if we wish to investigate the factors influencing 'studying behaviour' in the library we need to specify what we mean by 'studying behaviour' in order to measure it. We might decide on time actually spent reading as against chatting, looking round or dozing. In this example time spent reading will be our dependent variable.

The factors which influence studying behaviour are known as the *independent variables* and may be numerous. But let us say that we have observed that a number of other students present appears to have the most effect on 'studying behaviour'. In deciding to investigate the effect of this variable, we cannot just ignore the possible effects of the other variables. In order to demonstrate that number of students present effects studying behaviour, we must attempt to *control* the effects of these other variables so that their effect is cancelled out or kept constant throughout the experiment. In this example, two obvious variables we would need to control are room temperature and lighting intensity, and we would control them by keeping them constant. Similarly, when we select the subjects for our experiment we must also control for differences between them.

Having decided to keep our experiment simple, we have arrived at a simple two-group design to test our simplified hypothesis that a person alone in the library will engage in more studying behaviour than when he is in the company of other students. One group of students will study for one hour on their own in the library whereas the other group will study in a crowded library. Even this simple experiment could be tackled in many ways: for example, by having the same students, at different times, studying alone and also in a group, but we will not go into the complexities of these procedures here. We will keep our two groups distinct but we do need to know that they are comparable. If we suspect that girls engage in studying behaviour more than boys or *vice versa* we will make sure that we have equal numbers of each sex in both groups. But what about individual differences such as personality which might affect studying behaviour? In this case we would attempt to control for its effect by *randomization*, i.e. we would allocate subjects to the two groups randomly, which should guard against one group being substantially different from the other in terms of personality. It would obviously be silly to put all the quiet, serious subjects in the 'solitary' condition and all the noisy, gregarious ones in the 'crowded' condition. If we did this the effect of our independent variable, solitary/crowded conditions, would be *confounded* by the uncontrolled variable of personality and we would not know for sure what had caused the difference, if any, between the two groups.

These are not the only variables we would need to control in our experiment and doubtless the reader could suggest many more potential sources of influence which we have not ruled out.

But given that we have employed all the necessary controls, what then? The subjects will have been allocated to one of the groups and the amount of time each subject spent actually reading in the one-hour period will have been recorded. We then have two sets of numbers; the reading times for the solitary group and the crowded group. The most likely way of comparing the two groups is by comparing the average or *mean* time spent reading for the two groups. A statistical technique known as a *significance test* will enable us to compare the difference between the two means and to decide whether the difference is greater than we would expect due to chance or random variation. In this example we might find that solitary readers spend considerably more time actually reading, a result which might occur *by chance* less than once in a hundred similar experiments; this result would be said to be *statistically significant*.

The above is an example of the experimental method: a research technique which is based on deliberately manipulating the independent variable to determine its effect(s) on the dependent variable. It is an extremely powerful technique which allows the experimenter to feel confident that he has established a causal relationship between the independent and dependent variables if his manipulation of the independent variable has significantly effected the dependent variable. The experimental approach may be said to be very strong in terms of control but is often weak in terms of the randomization. This is because the highly controlled procedures can be very time-consuming, allowing only relatively few subjects to be given the task. These few subjects may not be enough to ensure that such factors as personality differences are in fact randomly distributed.

Non-experimental methods, on the other hand, commonly use very large samples and thus may be strong on randomization but they are usually weak in terms of control. Examples of non-experimental methods include surveys, field studies, observational techniques and correlation procedures. In these approaches the independent variable is not systematically manipulated. Data is collected about different aspects of the behaviour and the conditions under which it occurs, and attempts are made to relate the behaviour to the conditions. This is commonly carried out by measuring the *correlation* of two variables. Correlation is a means of measuring how well two variables relate to each other or go together. If we measured the height and weight of a sample of children we would expect that, overall, taller children would tend to be heavier. By computing a *correlation coefficient* we would have a statistical means of evaluating how close the relationship is. Correlation coefficients may also be tested for statistical significance, i.e. whether they are likely to have arisen by chance.

The important thing we must bear in mind about correlations, however, is the assumption of causality. Just because two variables correlate very highly does not mean that one causes the other. Weight does not cause height, nor does height cause weight, but they are both highly correlated with age. Increasing age may be said, in a sense, to cause increases in height and weight. Similarly, we might find that for a sample of students the number of books read per year correlated negatively with number of parties attended per year. This would mean that there was a relationship showing that a person who read many books attended few parties and a person who read few books attended many parties. Although one might try to make a case for a causal link between the two on the grounds that if you read a lot you do not have time for parties and if you go to lots of parties you do not have time to read, there is a more likely related variable which causes both, i.e. personality type. A quiet, thoughtful person who prefers his own company is likely to read a lot and avoid parties, whereas a more outgoing, socially inclined person is likely to read less and delight in parties.

Another point that must be clarified with regard to statistical evaluation of results is the nature of significance. Inherent in the design of statistical tests is an allowance for the size of sample used in the experiment or study. The effect of this is that, when large samples are employed, small numerical differences between means or low correlations may achieve statistical significance. The point to bear in mind is that although such results have been shown to be statistically significant, they are not necessarily psychologically significant, i.e. the variable may have been shown to have an effect but the size of the effect is so small that it tells us very little about the determinants of behaviour.

Whilst discussing methods in social psychology we should also bear in mind the social psychology of the experiment. By this I mean the social forces influencing the behaviour of individuals who take part in psychological experiments. The mere fact that we know that we are taking part in an experiment may

24

drastically alter our behaviour. This is one reason why many social psychologists prefer to run experiments in real-life situations but, as we have already said, this almost always leads to less control over the relevant variables. Laboratory studies, although more tightly controlled, are so prone to criticism on the grounds that the artificial situation generates artificial behaviour that there is now an extensive literature on the *demand characteristics* of the experimental situation (Orne 1962). The problem is summarized by Seltiz (1959):

If people feel that they are guinea pigs being experimented with or they feel that they are being 'tested' and must make a good impression, or if the method of data collection suggests responses or stimulates an interest the subjects did not previously feel, the measuring process may distort the results.

Swingle (1973) notes that the effect of this sort of contamination is difficult to assess, varying between subjects and situations.

It may vary from the subject's simply being somewhat less active or more uninhibited than usual in his behaviour ... to a situation in which he acts in exact contradiction of his own personal beliefs in an attempt to behave in a manner he thinks is appropriate. Thus an individual may act in a way he thinks the experimenter wants him to act, or in a way he feels normal people should act, but not the way he would behave were he unaware that his behaviour was being observed.

Orne (1962) has been mainly concerned with the effect of the subject knowing that he is taking part in an experiment on his behaviour. He maintains that the subject role is well understood so that, 'once a subject has agreed to participate in a psychological experiment, he implicitly agrees to perform a very wide range of actions on request without enquiring as to their purpose and frequently without enquiring as to their duration'. As examples of this he cites two instances. He found that if he asked casual acquaintances to do some push-ups for him as a favour, he was met with an incredulous 'Why?'. However, when he asked a similar group of people to take part in an experiment and, upon their agreement, then asked them to do some push-ups, the typical response was 'Where?'.

Similarly, he attempted to devise tasks which were 'psychologically noxious, meaningless or boring'. One of these consisted of performing a virtually unending series of simple additions. The subject, deprived of his watch, was asked to continue working until the experimenter returned. As Orne puts it, 'Five and one-half hours later, the experimenter gave up!'. This was by no means an isolated example. Further studies increased the meaninglessness of the task but subjects continued to persist at the task for hours with 'relatively little sign of overt hostility'.

In addition to this incredible diligence found in experimental subjects, Orne found a 'high regard for the aims of science and experimentation'. Subjects were very concerned to be 'good subjects', whose behaviour fitted in with what they perceived the experimental hypothesis to be.

Viewed in this way, the student volunteer is not merely a passive responder in an experimental situation but rather he has a very real stake in the successful outcome of the experiment. This problem is implicitly recognized in the large number of psychological studies which attempt to conceal the true purpose of the experiment from the subject in the hope of thereby obtaining more reliable data. This manoeuvre on the part of the psychologists is so widely known in the college population that even if a psychologist is honest with the subject, more often than not he will be distrusted. As one subject pithily put it, 'Psychologists always lie!'. This bit of paranoia has some support in reality. (Orne, 1962)

Orne considers that the subject's performance may be seen as a form of problem-solving behaviour whereby he puts together all the cues he can pick up in an attempt to divine the true purpose of the experiment. Such cues will include campus rumour, what the experimenter has actually said, the subject's previous experience and knowledge, etc. He reports that, in one study, only the students who had guessed and could verbalize the experimental hypothesis behaved in the way predicted; those who did not guess did not behave in the predicted way.

We will return to this problem of attempting to keep the real nature of the experiment from the subjects later in this chapter when we will consider the ethical implications of such procedures. There is, however, another potential source of bias other than the subjects: the experimenter himself. Rosenthal has conducted a lengthy programme of research into *expectancy effects*. We have all heard of the 'self-fulfilling prophecy'; an example would be of a person who is convinced that he will not

26

get the job for which he is being interviewed. On arriving at the interview he makes his prediction come true by behaving in such a way that no one in their right mind would ever employ him. Rosenthal's work suggests that experimenters influence their experiments in various ways to confirm their predictions. This may be carried out in various ways of which the experimenter is probably unaware. He may be inadvertently acknowledging the sort of responses he is predicting by nodding or showing visible relief when the subject behaves as he expected. The classic case is that of Clever Hans, a horse who could apparently figure out mathematical problems and give the correct answer by tapping with his foot the appropriate number. A more detailed study of the set up, however, revealed that Hans was smart, but not in terms of mathematical ability. When the problem was set, for example, two plus two, the horse would begin to tap and would stop tapping when he reached four, not because he could count, but because his master or even the experimenter would have inadvertently signalled when to stop by raising his head or by some other clue to which the horse had learned to respond.

Rosenthal (1966) demonstrated a similar phenomenon in an experiment in which his subjects acted as experimenters. One group were told that the rats they would be studying were from a strain of rats who were 'bright', i.e. who were bred from rats who performed well in psychological experiments, whereas the other group were told that their rats were 'dull'. In actual fact all the rats were just ordinary rats from the same laboratory stock. When the 'experimenters' studied the maze-running of their rats, they did indeed find differences; the bright rats apparently performed better than the dull rats. In that there was no real difference between the rats, it showed that expectancy by the experimenter does indeed influence the outcome of experiments.

Further studies showed that sex of the experimenter was also extremely important; male experimenters tended to interact with subjects in a much friendlier way, especially towards female subjects. The importance of experimenter effects in general will become even more clear when we look at operant verbal conditioning and non-verbal communication in Chapter 3, both of which provide partial explanations of how experimenters influence subjects. But how do we avoid this sort of effect? The answer is even greater control of experiments. Tape-recorded or written instructions to subjects is one way of avoiding sex differentiation and the inadvertent giving of clues. Another technique is to use experimenters who themselves do not know all the details of the experiment. It would be preferable if the experimenter was not aware of the hypothesis being tested but if this cannot be achieved he can at least be kept in ignorance of the experimental group of which his subjects are members.

In considering these possible sources of contamination in social psychological research we should also exercise discretion in the implications we draw from social psychological experiments. One major factor is whether the findings apply to anyone but the subjects studied in the experiment, for instance to people from other cultures. This is particularly pertinent as a great deal of the research in social psychology, and indeed in psychology generally, has been carried out in one culture, the United States. Findings regarding social phenomena established in the United States are not necessarily universal. We cannot assume that British policemen would victimize subjects driving cars bearing 'Angry Brigade' stickers. The idiosyncratically American way of life, its culture and values, will influence research findings which may not generalize to similar western cultures, let alone non-western cultures. The specificity of research findings may be even more extreme; the population studied in many experiments tends to be Mid-Western college students. Consequently, demonstrations that people are aggressive, conforming or competitive are less spectacular if we remember the population and culture studied. We must not assume that we are finding out about 'universal man'. It is more likely that the behaviour we are observing is a manifestation of the values of the culture to which our subjects belong. An American college student will be encouraged to be competitive but in some North American Indian tribes, for example, competitiveness is seen as the height of bad manners.

Finally, I have a confession to make. If I was asked to take part as a subject in a social psychological experiment I would be extremely reluctant to agree. Why? Because social psychologists are rapidly becoming the biggest bunch of con-men working under the name of science! As Swingle (1973) puts it:

Subjects have been exposed to deceptive manipulations that have led them to believe that they had exposed a helpless person to extremely painful shock or loud noise, were homosexually aroused, had cheated, lied, or yielded. Persons have been observed to cheat, to open and keep lost mail, and to lie. Experimenters have joined groups and pretended to share the group's norms and beliefs in order to observe the behaviour of gangs, religious extremists and work crews. Washrooms have been bugged, private conversations have been recorded, audiences in darkened theatres have been observed with infrared systems, and researchers have hidden under beds in students' dormitory rooms to record conversations during tea parties.

The reason for most of these bizarre activities is to attempt to get round the problem of demand characteristics. But whilst approving of the ingenuity employed and agreeing with the need to make the experiment as watertight as possible, we must not forget the ethics of this sort of research.

Many people feel that it is morally wrong to carry out experiments which involve pain or death to dumb animals. On the other hand, vivisectionists would argue that if, for example, new drugs or new surgical techniques were not tried out on animals first then we would either have to experiment on human beings or do without the potential but untested life-savers or pain-relievers: surely it is morally right to reduce pain in human beings even if it involves pain being inflicted on animals. Luckily, few if any experiments in social psychology involve any possibility of severe physical pain or danger to the subjects, but the possibility of psychological distress being incurred does exist. Is the risk of this justified by our demands for greater knowledge of social phenomena? McGuire (1972) makes the point that it is also unethical to carry out bad research:

The psychological researcher is obligated to do good and ethical research. Hence, it is morally reprehensible to do unethical research; but it is also morally reprehensible to do bad research or no research.

He also points out the existentialist argument that 'the decision not to act is an act that may be morally reprehensible'.

At the very lowest level, being fooled is not a pleasant experience. Imagine, then, what it must feel like to know that you have been observed to behave in a way of which you would normally disapprove (e.g. the subjects in the obedience studies reported in Chapter 5). The social psychologist's answer to this

29

is careful *de-briefing* in which the subject is finally told the real purpose of the experiment and is reassured that the whole thing is confidential and that he is not to worry, etc. Unfortunately, de-briefing could be even more humiliating, especially if it were carried out inexpertly or as a matter of routine.

Similarly, deception in order to disguise the purpose of the experiment and spying on a subject who does not know that he is being observed are both seen by some as morally reprehensible. The critics of such techniques offer *role-playing* as an alternative. This involves explaining to the subject the purpose of the experiment and then asking him to take part by acting normally, as if he did not know the purpose of the experiment. The absurdity of this technique is perhaps less than it appears but it does sound as if the experimenter is virtually saying, 'This is the experiment. What do you think the result will be?' Perhaps in my own research on sentence-comprehension in mentally handicapped children I could have extended this technique and avoided inflicting boredom on these children by hiring an actor to role-play the responses of the hundreds of children I tested!

The basic problem remains, however. How do you obtain accurate, uncontaminated data about socially relevant phenomena without treading on ethical toes? Basically, it must resolve itself by being left in the hands of the individual experimenter who is, after all, a professional.

Having detected the morally reprehensible aspects of the work, the researcher should evaluate the costs and gains of doing the research versus not doing it, or of continuing to do it with the reprehensible aspect versus some substituted procedure.

(McGuire, 1972)

Ethical considerations also come into decisions as to whether certain sorts of research should be carried out and, if they are, how they should be reported. There has been considerable recent controversy surrounding the names of Jensen and Eysenck, who have dared to carry out research on racial differences in intelligence. Their conclusion is that black people on average score fifteen points lower on I.Q. tests than whites. The controversy is by no means clear cut, as it includes several related issues, argued both by scientists and laymen, many of whom seem to be, or choose to be, unaware of the facts. Putting on one side the considerable theoretical criticism of the research, there still remain the ethical considerations. Some critics argue that the research should never have been carried out, but given that it had, should not have been published or at least not released to the popular press and news media. The scientists carrying out the research maintain, perhaps naively, that their concern is merely to demonstrate the heritability of intelligence. For this, they are branded as fascists by the left. Eysenck, in particular, has been banned from speaking at universities by the National Union of Students.

Thus the social psychologist's task is becoming increasingly difficult. There is a demand that his research be socially relevant but he must not use unethical techniques such as deception in order to get uncontaminated data. Moreover, it now appears that he must also carefully consider the possible political repercussions of his research. Brozek (1966) reports that the whole of early Soviet social psychology was liquidated by the ideologists who saw social psychology as a 'monopoly of bourgeois psychologists and sociologists' (Filatov, cited by Brozek). Apparently ideology still dominates social psychology as the following quotation from a research report by Bashilov *et al.* (cited by Brozek) shows:

Bourgeois science, in its endeavour to fight Marxism, psychologizes social phenomena. Soviet psychologists, having totally rejected the theory of bourgeois social psychology, can accept some of its concrete investigations. It has become essential at present to develop a Marxist social psychology.

Whilst bearing in mind these considerations, it would, however, be a tragedy if the potential scope of social psychology was limited only to politically sterile topics and to procedures and techniques which are ethically neutral. It is vital that we remain free to attempt to gain further insight into all forms of social behaviour, both for academic reasons and also for the possible applications which may result from a greater understanding of social phenomena. In order to change society for the better we must first understand the forces controlling social behaviour.

2
Social learning

Scientific psychology as against philosophical psychology is basically concerned with empirically establishing the causes and effects of behaviour. As we have seen, there has been a movement away from attributing behaviours to innate properties to a concern with how behaviours are learned. The early learning theorists' claims, often somewhat dogmatic and extreme, faced considerable opposition from those who saw behaviourism as a denial of free will; determinism was seen as denying the basic human-ness of human beings. Later theorists, however, adopting more caution and perhaps more diplomacy, demonstrated by careful experimentation and sophisticated models of 'conditioning', that learning is probably the most important determinant of behaviour, not only of animal behaviour but also of human behaviour (see A3). We are concerned in this chapter to examine the use of various types of learning theory to answer the question 'how is social behaviour acquired?'

It has been said that all scientific psychologists are now behaviourists. Although many would quarrel with this, nearly all psychologists agree on the importance of learning as a determinant of human behaviour. The role of operant conditioning in particular is now seen by many as being critical in making us as we are. It must be made clear, however, that some psychologists, whilst accepting the evidence for operant learning, are dissatisfied with the current accounts of its operating principles. They are prepared to believe the evidence that it works, and many will use the methods, but remain dissatisfied with the explanations given of why it works. Such critics claim that operant psychologists are not providing causal explanations at all; at best, they say, their accounts are merely descriptive and often, which is worse, tautologous. But rather than going into technicalities about this we must first establish what the basic principles of learning appear to be. This is important to our study of social psychology as social behaviour because learning, as we shall see throughout the book, influences social behaviour just like any other behaviour. It should perhaps be emphasized that some social psychologists, whilst recognizing the importance of learning, nevertheless tend to ignore it in their formulations or prefer to adopt a larger-scale approach in their theories of social behaviour. I can personally see some value in the latter approach but I also feel that it is as well to keep one's feet on the ground and constantly to bear in mind the basic influences affecting behaviour, especially learning.

The account of learning or 'conditioning' theories given here is greatly simplified. Basically I will be making a distinction between *classical conditioning* and *operant conditioning* associated with the names of Pavlov (1927) and Skinner (1953) respectively. Obviously there are many more theories of learning than these, differing from each other to a greater or lesser degree, but it would be far beyond the scope of this book even to mention them. We will, however, discuss learning by *imitation*.

Classical conditioning (see A3)

The paradigm of classical conditioning was initially demonstrated by the famous Russian physiologist I. P. Pavlov. Pavlov was carrying out a series of experiments which involved measuring the amount of saliva produced by a dog when given food. The act of salivation to food is an example of a reflex – an involuntary, predictable, unlearned response to a stimulus, in this case food. The knee-jerk reflex is another example. One does not learn to jerk one's knee when it is tapped, nor can one stop it jerking. Reflexes are innate and appear to be 'pre-wired' systems which serve the body in some way – salivation to food aids digestion, for example.

Whilst carrying out his investigations into salivation, Pavlov noticed that sometimes the dogs began to salivate before being presented with the food. The sight of the man who normally fed them, or even the sound of his footsteps, was enough to cause salivation to begin, in anticipation of the food. This observation resulted in Pavlov's discovery of the *conditioned reflex*. His experimental procedures showed that almost any event associated with the presentation of food would eventually elicit salivation in the absence of food. His most famous demonstration made use of a bell which was repeatedly sounded just prior to the presentation of food which resulted in the salivation reflex. Eventually the bell alone was sufficient to elicit salivation. The salivation reflex was now occurring in response to a new stimulus, the bell. A stimulus-response link had been established which was not innate, for if the bell had never been presented before the food it would never have elicited the salivation. He termed the salivation to the bell a conditioned reflex. Now we have the basic classical conditioning paradigm which we can express in 'trade jargon'. The food is known as the unconditioned stimulus because it elicits salivation, the unconditioned response, without any prior conditioning. This stimulus-response link is innate. The bell is known as the conditioned stimulus because it will only elicit salivation when it has previously been successively presented prior to the food being given, i.e. it only functions as a stimulus to salivation when it has been conditioned to do so. Salivation in response to the conditioned stimulus, the bell, is known as the conditioned response since the response would not have been elicited by the bell alone prior to conditioning. Another example of this is the innate unconditioned reflex of eye-blink to a puff of air directed at the eyeball. Successive presentations of a tone (the conditioned stimulus) prior to the puff of air (the unconditioned stimulus) resulting in the eye-blink response (the unconditioned response) will eventually result in the tone alone eliciting the eye-blink response (the conditioned response).

An important effect found in classical conditioning is that of *stimulus generalization*. Given that a tone of a certain frequency has been established as a conditioned stimulus, what happens if you present a lower or higher tone? The answer is that the conditioning generalizes to similar stimuli so that higher or lower tones of a similar frequency will also elicit the conditioned response. The response decreases, however, as the stimulus becomes more dissimilar to the original conditioned stimulus. This

34

means that if we established a red light as a conditioned stimulus eliciting the eye-blink response, we might also succeed with an orange light but probably not with a yellow light. It follows logically from this that we now have a means of testing how similar two stimuli are as perceived by the subject, be he animal or human, by the degree of generalization of response from one to the other stimulus.

What happens if we continue to elicit the response with the conditioned stimulus, however? Is the conditioned link permanent when once established? These questions lead us to the phenomenon of *extinction*. If a conditioned stimulus is continually used to elicit the conditioned response without ever again pairing it with the original unconditioned stimulus, the response becomes less likely to be elicited by the conditioned stimulus, in other words it extinguishes. So, if we keep on ringing the bell and not presenting food, the dog will eventually stop salivating to the bell. The extinguished response can be rapidly re-established, however, by once more pairing the conditioned stimulus, the bell, with the unconditioned stimulus, the food.

By now, the reader, weary of this technical detail, must be saying 'O.K. if I want to train my cat to come for its dinner when I whistle, I'll bear classical conditioning in mind, but what has it got to do with people in the real world?' George Bernard Shaw certainly thought he knew the answer to this question. He saw Pavlov and his work as a very real threat; a means by which people could be conditioned into conformity. What Shaw was ignoring, however, in company with contemporary critics, is that conditioning is not an unnatural process dreamed up in a laboratory but a discovery of one of the basic laws by which we all learn. We shall return to this theme again later in this chapter but first let us examine some everyday examples of classical conditioning. If a dog bites a small child, causing him to cry, the mere sight of the dog may be sufficient to make him cry on subsequent occasions; moreover it is often the case that he will become frightened of all dogs, demonstrating stimulus generalization.

An applied use of classical conditioning is said to exist in the technique of *aversion therapy*, an application which might well have justified Shaw's fears of a potential 1984-type society. If you have read or seen the film of *A Clockwork Orange*, the 'Reclamation Treatment' ('Ludoviko's technique') which is used to eliminate Alex's violent behaviour might remind you of aversion therapy. It has been used, apparently successfully, on homosexuals, alcoholics, drug-addicts and other problem cases society sees fit to define as problem cases. (The temptation to discuss the ethics of this I will, regretfully, resist.)

Taking the treatment of a homosexual as an example, the procedure involves attempting to condition erotic homosexual emotions induced by nude male 'pin-ups' or films to feelings of pain/fear. The unconditioned reflex consists of a strong electric shock (the unconditioned stimulus) which elicits a pain/fear response (the unconditioned response). The response may be behaviourally observable as flinching or signalled by changes in certain physiological processes such as the rate of heart-beat or the perspiration level which may be measured by appropriate recording instruments. The 'pin-up', the conditioned stimulus, is presented just prior to the electric shock. After a series of treatments this results in the 'pin-up' becoming the conditioned stimulus eliciting the pain/fear response, the conditioned response, in the absence of the electric shock. This association of pain/fear with homosexually erotic material will, it is argued, militate against its arousing properties and will, it is hoped, generalize to live situations so that the homosexual will no longer be 'turned on' by men.

Classical conditioning can thus be seen to be a form of learning which occurs naturally in everyday life and which can also, when systematically applied, be used as an efficient means of changing certain behaviours.

Operant conditioning (see A3)

Unlike classical conditioning, operant conditioning is not restricted to physiological, autonomic responses. It does not build on innate established stimulus-response links but can be used to build up complex behaviour by the conditioning of simple discrete responses which the animal emits.

Skinner makes a distinction between responses which are elicited by a stimulus as in reflexes and those which are emitted without any known stimulus. The former type of responses are known as *respondents*, the latter type as *operants*. Skinner's concern was (a) to show that the emission of operants could be controlled, as exampled by increasing the rate of emission, and (b) to determine what variables affected the rate of emission. Skinner carried out most of his early work with pigeons, one of which would typically be placed in a small, sound-proofed box, now known in the trade as a Skinner box. Inside one of these boxes a lever is positioned on one wall and underneath it a food tray into which food pellets may be released. Typically the pigeon, who will usually be in a hungry state, will wander about, perhaps first pecking the floor, then the wall and eventually, by chance, the lever. This will immediately result in a pellet of food being released which will be rapidly consumed by the hungry pigeon. If we continue to watch the pigeon we will notice that the frequency of lever pressing by the pigeon will increase. Skinner (1953), avoiding the jargon and 'explanatory fiction' of earlier theorists, describes this process objectively:

We make a given consequence contingent upon certain physical properties of behaviour (in our case pecking the lever), and the behaviour is then observed to increase in frequency.

Following Pavlov in his analysis of the conditioned reflex, Skinner adopted the term *reinforcement* to refer to any event which strengthened behaviour.

In operant conditioning we 'strengthen' an operant in the sense of making a response more possible or, in actual fact, more frequent.... In the pigeon experiment ... food is the *reinforcer* and presenting food when a response is emitted is the reinforcement. The operant is defined by the property upon which the reinforcement is contingent. (Skinner, 1953)

Skinner's theory of learning basically argues that most behaviour consists of the emission of operant responses in the absence of known stimuli. The rate of emission of an operant will increase if the operant is reinforced, for example, by giving a hungry animal food. Reinforcers are very difficult to define but are basically stimuli that the animal will seek out. Hence, food will reinforce a hungry animal, and sexual gratification and the alleviation of thirst may also function as reinforcers. These are examples of *unconditioned positive reinforcers* in that, as they appear to be innate, they may be said to be unconditioned and, in that, as the animal will seek them out, they may be said to be positive. *Negative reinforcers* consist of stimuli that the animal will seek to avoid, the termination of which will be reinforcing, such as an electric shock which will reinforce behaviour by its removal. Hence an animal's bar-pressing behaviour may be reinforced positively by giving it food or negatively by terminating an electric shock. Negative reinforcement sounds like *punishment* but the two are by no means the same. Negative reinforcement has the effect of increasing responses by the termination of an aversive stimulus whereas punishment consists of presenting the aversive stimulus in an attempt to reduce the frequency of responses. Skinner considers punishment to be a rather unreliable and time-consuming way of preventing responses from occurring and does not give it much emphasis in his writings. In passing, we should note that removing positive reinforcers is also a form of punishment.

The only satisfactory way of defining reinforcers, therefore, is in terms of their effects or operations. Hence, an *operational definition* of a reinforcer might be: a reinforcer consists of any stimulus which, when following an operant, has the effect of increasing the probability of the occurrence of that operant in the future.

Behaviour which has been operantly conditioned is also susceptible to extinction and generalization in much the same way as behaviour which has been classically conditioned. If you stop reinforcing the animal for pecking the bar, his rate of pecking will go down and eventually extinguish completely. There are ways round this, however, which can be achieved by varying the rate at which the animal is reinforced. So far we have only considered the example of reinforcing the animal every time he presses the bar. This is known as the schedule of *continuous reinforcement* and is often used to establish the behaviour initially. Once established, however, we may move on to more complex *schedules of reinforcements*. One may vary the rate of dispensing reinforcers in relation to the *number* of responses emitted, e.g. give a reinforcer every five bar-presses, or vary the rate of dispensing reinforcers according to a set *time* interval, e.g. give a reinforcer every ten seconds. The former is called a *ratio schedule* and the latter is called an *interval schedule*. Similarly, each of these two kinds of schedule may be *fixed* or *variable*. In a *fixed-ratio* schedule the animal will be given a reinforcer every X responses. In a *variable-ratio* schedule the animal will be reinforced after different numbers of responses on different occasions. So a fixed ratio 10 schedule means that the animal will be reinforced after every 10 responses but a variable ratio 10 schedule means that he may be reinforced after 5 responses the first time, 15 responses the second, 10 responses the third etc., which will eventually average out at 10 responses per reinforcer. The same distinction applies between *fixed-interval* and *variable-interval* schedules. On a fixed-interval 30-second schedule, the animal will consistently be reinforced following the first response to occur after each 30-second interval, regardless of how many bar-presses the animal has emitted. On a variable-interval 30-second schedule, however, the size of interval varies, sometimes being smaller and sometimes being greater than 30 seconds but the average interval will equal 30 seconds.

But why do we need to know about the technicalities of scheduling? Simply because different schedules produce different effects. Without going into these in detail, a few generalizations will demonstrate the point of all this. In terms of efficiency we can get more responses for fewer reinforcers by employing any one of the above schedules in preference to continuous reinforcement, i.e. we can get more bar-presses for less food. Moreover, resistance to extinction is greater using these schedules, i.e. the animal will continue to bar-press for longer after we stop reinforcing it. The variable-ratio schedule is particularly efficient in both these respects in that it can produce very rapid bar-pressing which will not extinguish quickly. If the ratio is high enough it is even possible to get the animal working so hard that the energy it expends in bar-pressing is more than it will obtain from the food reinforcers which it receives only occasionally.

Generalization as well as extinction may be observed in operantly conditioned behaviour. Although Skinner's definition of operants refers to responses being emitted without any known stimuli, responses may be placed under *stimulus control*, i.e. so that they will occur under certain stimulus conditions and not under others. If we reinforce a pigeon for bar-pressing when a red light is on but not when a green light is on, the pigeon's bar-pressing under the green light will extinguish, whereas his rate of bar-pressing to the red light will increase. Thus the pigeon will have learned to discriminate between the two colours. The stimulus to which the pigeon will bar-press, having been conditioned to do so, is known as the *discriminative stimulus*. The effect of the discriminative stimulus may well generalize to similar stimuli. Hence we can show stimulus generalization by demonstrating that the pigeon will bar-press under an orange light but probably not under a yellow light, which is less similar to the red but more similar to the green light under which reinforcement was not given.

Skinner's approach as presented so far may appear only to account for the learning of simple behaviour by animals but his theory and method of *shaping* shows that it may equally well account for more complex behaviour. Skinner argues that we can build up more complex behaviour by successively reinforcing closer and closer approximations to the desired target behaviour. If we wish to get a pigeon to peck at a target spot on the wall of the experimental box we could wait for the appropriate free operant to occur at random and then reinforce it. This could involve a lengthy wait, however, and the pigeon might never emit that specific operant. Instead we would proceed in the following manner.

We first give the bird food when it turns slightly in the direction of the spot from any part of the cage. This increases the frequency of such behaviour. We then withhold reinforcement until a slight movement is made towards the spot. This again alters the general distribution of behaviour without producing a new unit. We continue by reinforcing positions successively closer to the spot, then by reinforcing only when the head is moved slightly forward, and finally only when the beak actually makes contact with the spot. We may reach this final response in a remarkably short time. A hungry bird, well adapted to the situation and to the food tray, can usually be brought to respond in this way in two or three minutes.... By reinforcing a series of successive approximations, we bring a rare response to a very high probability in a short time. (Skinner, 1953)

Similarly Skinner has demonstrated in front of audiences how a naive pigeon may be shaped into walking a figure of eight course and has even trained pairs of pigeons to play a version of ping-pong with their beaks! But this is again only emphasizing experimental control over behaviour. Skinner's argument is that this is how learning takes place in real life. There does not have to be an agent who dispenses reinforcement to a previously determined procedure. This is exampled by the phenomenon of *superstitious behaviour* which occurs as a result of *accidental*

40

learning. Suppose we had no pre-determined behaviour in view but reinforced the pigeon every fifteen seconds regardless of what it was doing. The important thing is that it must have been doing something when it was reinforced and consequently the behaviour will be more likely to occur again as it has been reinforced. From this it follows that the probability of it again being reinforced for the same behaviour is also greater and consequently we can shortly expect to see the pigeon performing a highly specific behaviour for which it is receiving reinforcement although no one has planned it. This can result in such bizarre behaviours as hopping from one foot to the other or bowing and scraping.

I trust the reader's patience has not been stretched too far by this lengthy discourse on pigeons learning to peck appropriately but the reason for it will, I hope, become clear as we move on to discuss *conditioned reinforcers*, which will rapidly take us away from pigeons and back amongst people. Reinforcers can themselves be conditioned, by which I mean that a stimulus which occurs in the presence of a reinforcer will itself acquire reinforcing properties if it is continually paired with the reinforcer. Getting back to our pigeons, we can demonstrate that if we turn on a light every time we dispense a food pellet, the light itself will soon become a conditioned reinforcer. It will rapidly lose its reinforcing properties, however, if we withhold food.

A most important conditioned reinforcer is money, which is an example of a *token*. Other tokens include marks or grades in school, diplomas, medals etc., which although they cannot directly be used to purchase primary reinforcers may indirectly aid their future acquisition.

Money can usually be directly exchanged for primary unconditioned reinforcers – if you have money it is unlikely that you will ever starve.

Many of the most important reinforcers controlling human behaviour are conditioned but are, nevertheless, extremely powerful. The first of these is *attention*, which rapidly becomes a conditioned reinforcer.

The attention of people is reinforcing because it is a necessary condition for other reinforcements from them. In general only people who are attending to us reinforce our behaviour. The attention of someone who is particularly likely to supply reinforcement – a parent, a teacher or a loved one – is an especially

41

good generalized reinforcer and sets up especially strong attention getting behaviour. (Skinner, 1953)

A related and equally powerful conditioned reinforcer is *approval*. People tend to reinforce only those aspects of a person's behaviour of which they approve and hence any symbol of approval such as a smile or a 'That's super' becomes a reinforcer.

Verbal reinforcers derive their power from the specific reinforcers with which they are used, and since they are used with different reinforcers from time to time, the effect may be generalized. We reinforce a person positively by saying 'Good!' or 'Right!' and negatively by saying 'Bad!' or 'Wrong!' and these verbal stimuli are effective because they have been accompanied by other reinforcers. (Skinner, 1971)

Similarly, there is the very powerful conditioned reinforcer of *affection* which Skinner suggests may primarily derive its power from its association with sexual contact but which becomes generalized when associated with other kinds of reinforcement.

Reinforcers which require the presence of other people are known as *social reinforcers*. Attention, approval and affection are all social reinforcers. There are also conditioned, social, negative reinforcers which consist of the presentation by others of aversive stimuli. These include signs of disapproval, disgust, contempt, ridicule, insult, etc., and reinforce behaviour by their termination. Small boys and some small-minded men make use of continual jeering until the victim eventually does what they want him to do whereupon the jeering stops. Unfortunately, the jeering behaviour, like blackmailing, is itself reinforced by the fact that it has got the jeerers/blackmailers what they want.

The strength of attention as a conditioned social reinforcer is demonstrated by its removal in the following study. Williams (1959) reported the case of a twenty-one-month-old child who was causing his parents considerable anxiety by continually throwing tantrums in order to get what he wanted. This was especially prevalent at bedtime.

If the parents left the bedroom ... S [the child] would scream and fuss until the parents returned. ... If the parents began to read while in the bedroom, S would cry until the reading material was put down. The parents felt that S enjoyed his control over them and that he fought off going to sleep as long as he could. In any event, a parent was spending from one-half to two hours each bedtime just waiting in the bedroom until S went to sleep.

This dilemma was resolved quite simply. The parents instigated a new bedtime procedure. After the child was put to bed, the parent said good-night, left the room and closed the door. Initially, of course, this resulted in the child throwing a scream-

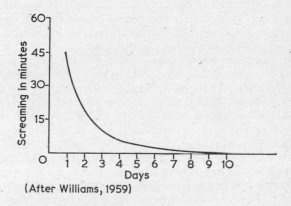

(After Williams, 1959)

Fig. 1 *A simplified extinction curve for the reduction of screaming behaviour*

ing tantrum which was ignored by the parents who merely recorded its duration. The change in behaviour was dramatic. A solid forty-five minutes' screaming was recorded on the first day of the new procedure but by day seven the screaming had stopped completely. This is an example of extinction. Figure 1 shows a simplified *extinction curve* for the reduction of screaming behaviour.

Thus we can see that once we stop reinforcing the child for screaming by withdrawing the social reinforcement of attention the screaming behaviour extinguishes.

Few parents seem to realize that they often bring tantrum

troubles upon themselves. How often have we observed the following incident in a shopping precinct? A toddler passing a shop window with his mother sees a toy or lollipop and shouts, 'I wannit, I wannit!' Mother says, 'Not today dear' and moves on. The child stays behind, begins to stamp his feet and repeats his demand more and more volubly. Eventually the mother smacks the child in desperation, which immediately results in a screaming fit. The embarrassed mother gives in and buys the child the toy or the lollipop. The child beams triumphantly and the mother is only too glad that the incident is over. Unfortunately, of course, the problem has only just begun. The mother has quite definitely reinforced the screaming and demanding by giving the child a reward. The best solution to the problem is not to reinforce that behaviour in the first place but given that the problem exists the only remedy is to employ an extinction procedure, i.e. stop reinforcing the child by refusing to buy goodies in such situations. An ingenious mother will make 'goodies' contingent upon good behaviour throughout the shopping trip, i.e. the child will only get a present at the end if he behaves satisfactorily throughout. An even more ingenious mother, who has read the section on reinforcement schedules carefully, will realize that if she only reinforces 'being good at the shops' occasionally, then she will not only save money spent on lollipops but will also have brought good behaviour under greater control, for it will take longer to extinguish if the lollipops are eventually withheld altogether.

Mallott (1973), in his very amusing introduction to social reinforcement, argues that the social reinforcer of approval is very important in marijuana-smoking behaviour in young people.

I wouldn't deny that marijuana is a heavy unconditioned reinforcer. However, those who would deny that conditioned social reinforcement also plays a major part in marijuana consumption are fooling themselves. The Now Generation receives considerable conditioned social reinforcement for smoking grass and considerable conditioned social punishment for abstinence. Remember, social reinforcement and punishment can be subtle. Don't expect someone to slap you on the back and say you're the greatest thing going just because you puff a joint. You may only get a warm acceptance; but what more do you want? ... If you smoke dope you are exceptionally hip. The problem is that soon everyone on the campus will be smoking dope, then who can you be hippier than? ... Once everyone starts smoking marijuana, the conditioned social reinforcement for smoking it will decrease, just as it did for smoking straight cigarettes and drinking beer.

One suspects that hip jargon may also be under the control of social reinforcement. 'Far out', 'too much man', 'I really dig that', 'groovy', 'freaking', etc., are likely to increase in frequency if one 'raps' in these terms and they meet with social approval. Positive social reinforcement can really 'turn you on'. Operant verbal conditioning will be discussed in more detail in Chapter 3 on communication, but what about choice of clothes? Is it possible to condition clothes-wearing behaviour? The highly lucrative fashion industry suggests that this is more than likely and there is experimental evidence to back it up. Calvin (1962) arranged for his students to compliment all girls wearing blue in the lunch hour following classes. Before complimenting was introduced, 25 per cent of the girls were wearing blue but after five days of complimenting this had risen to 37 per cent. When complimenting was terminated, the percentage dropped back to 27 per cent.

The point of these examples is to demonstrate that operant conditioning is not only a technique which we can employ but is a general law of learning. It constitutes one of the ways in which we learn in the outside world when there is no experimenter controlling the reinforcers and schedules. Superstitious behaviour is an example of this. How often have we seen someone perform a fairly complicated sequence of behaviour which is apparently irrelevant to the end result? A person goes into a lift and presses the button four times, slaps the panel and stamps his foot. This form of superstitious behaviour has probably been conditioned. On at least one occasion in the past, the person has probably done this and the lift has appeared to start quicker, thereby reinforcing his behaviour. He is just like the pigeon in the Skinner box. You do not need to be aware of reinforcement contingencies to be conditioned. As Malott (1973) says:

Occasionally we are aware of the extent to which our behaviour is influenced by conditioned social reinforcement; more often we are not. Occasionally, we can recognize the extent to which our social approval is influencing and even controlling the behaviour of others, more often we would be shocked to learn

45

of such influences. We don't necessarily say to ourselves, 'I'm going to do such and such so as to get social approval' or 'If I approve and smile when a person does a particular thing, then he'll be more likely to do it the next time'. Awareness of the principles of behaviour as they relate to our own actions should help us deal more effectively with our social environment, but it is not a pre-requisite for our being affected by that environment.

Skinner is really only describing what we have always done to teach or change behaviour. Reward and punishment have always been used by those wishing to control behaviour – the parent, the teacher, the administrator. Good behaviour is rewarded, bad behaviour is punished. Skinner's principal contributions are in demonstrating the effectiveness of positive reinforcement, how it may be used efficiently and how reinforcers can only be defined by their effect on behaviour. He has demonstrated that this is a principal means by which animals, including man, learn, and how, by carefully controlling the contingencies, we can control behaviour.

Imitation

Whilst not disagreeing with the principles of operant conditioning, Bandura (1967) argues that it does not account for all learning. He agrees that operant learning accounts for behaviour already in the learner's repertoire but remains unconvinced by the operant explanation of the acquisition of novel behaviour by the learner. As we have seen, Skinner argues that more complex behaviour may be built up by shaping, but Bandura argues that very little social learning would take place if this lengthy procedure were necessary to learn each bit of new behaviour. Bandura maintains that much behaviour is learned by *imitation* or *modelling*, as he prefers to call it. This consists basically of learning by example.

Parental modeling behavior may often counteract the effects of their direct training. When a parent punishes his child physically for having aggressed towards peers, for example, the intended outcome of this training is that the child should refrain from hitting others. The child, however, is also learning from parental demonstration how to aggress physically and this imitative learning may provide the direction for the child's behaviour when he is similarly frustrated in subsequent social interactions.

Research bearing on modeling demonstrates that, unlike the relatively slow process of instrumental training, when a model is provided, patterns of behavior are rapidly acquired in large segments or in their entirety (Bandura, 1962). The pervasiveness of this form of learning is also clearly evident in naturalistic observations of children's play in which they frequently reproduce the entire parental role, including the appropriate mannerisms, voice inflections and attitudes, much to the parents' surprise and embarrassment. (Bandura, 1967)

Bandura does not, however, ignore the importance of reinforcement. The likely model, the parent or teacher, is also likely to be an important dispenser of reinforcement who will frequently socially reinforce approximations of their own behaviour. Experiments have demonstrated that this is the case; models are more likely to be imitated if they have the power to reinforce. My five-year-old son Robin and his friend Howard were watching T.V. Robin, on seeing an 'ape-man', began to leap up and down on his arm-chair. Howard, who was tempted to do the same, looked across at me. My request that Robin should sit down was almost immediately echoed by Howard, who obviously saw me as a more powerful source of reinforcement than his friend and, therefore, a preferable model.

Much of Bandura's work has been concerned with aggression and is in direct conflict with psychoanalytic interpretations. The traditional psychoanalyst's view of aggression is that it consists of pent up energy which is harmful. In order to lessen aggression they would advocate catharsis, a 'let it all hang out' approach, by aggressing directly or vicariously. Consequently he would argue that watching televised aggression or acting out aggressive games will serve to reduce aggression. Bandura and his co-workers, on the basis of their research, argue that this amounts to training people to be more aggressive by providing models and reinforcing aggressive behaviour. Providing examples of alternative, non-aggressive ways of dealing with frustration, however, leads to a reduction in aggressive behaviour.

This has obvious relevance to our current pre-occupation with the apparently general increase of violent behaviour in society ranging from muggings in New York to violence at football matches. Judging by their popularity, footballers must be powerful models for many young people. It is, therefore, not surprising that the increase in heavy tackling, outbursts of pique and fighting between players is quickly followed by dramatic increases in spectator violence resulting finally in murder on the football terraces. Bandura is particularly alarmed that the model does not even have to be experienced first-hand.

The finding that film-mediated models are as effective as real-life models in eliciting and transmitting aggressive responses indicates that televised models may serve as important sources of behaviour and can no longer be ignored in conceptualizations of personality development. Indeed, most youngsters probably have more exposure to televised male models than to their own fathers. With further advances in mass media and audio-visual technology, models presented pictorially, mainly through television, are likely to play an increasingly influential role in shaping personality patterns and in modifying attitudes and social norms.
(Bandura, 1967)

Imitation will be considered again in Chapter 4, showing how attitudes may be learned by imitation.

Conditioning and society

It certainly appears to be the case that imitation may account for a great deal of social learning backed up by appropriate reinforcement. As we engage in everyday life, interacting with other people, we are constantly reinforcing and being reinforced; we also imitate models who dispense reinforcers or whose behaviour is likely to be reinforced. Almost all social behaviour may be viewed in these terms and consequently social psychology may be seen as being primarily concerned with the process of social learning. Not all social psychologists would take this view, however, but it is an approach which is gaining in acceptance. It certainly appears to provide an explanation for many social phenomena.

Social psychologists are concerned with determining the causes and consequences of social behaviour. By establishing the factors which influence social behaviour we can begin to predict the likely outcome given the details of the situation. Following prediction, of course, comes the bogeyman of control. The very mention of the word control seems to send some people into paroxysms of self-righteousness. The use of psychology to control people is apparently a manifestly unspeakable evil, immediately associated with *1984*. But if we are cool about this and consider what happens in everyday life, we realize that we are constantly trying to predict and control other people's behaviour, even when we are not at the time aware of doing so. Similarly, we are also being controlled and having our behaviour modified.

This problem of 'mind control' turns up in Michael Crichton's science fiction novel, *The Terminal Man*, which I strongly recommend as an amusing yarn from which one can learn quite a bit about psychology. (But look out for the not-so-deliberate mistake when Crichton confuses punishment with negative reinforcement!) Having planted a mini-computer inside a man's head linked to his brain in an attempt to prevent fits accompanied by physical violence, the research team are accused of mind control:

The truth was that everybody's mind was controlled, and everybody was glad for it. The most powerful mind controllers in the world were parents and they did the most damage. Theorists usually forgot that nobody was born prejudiced, neurotic or hung up; those traits required a helping hand. Of course, parents didn't intentionally damage their children. They merely inculcated attitudes that they felt would be important and useful to their children.

New born children were little computers waiting to be programmed. And they would learn whatever they were taught, from bad grammar to bad attitudes.

The quarrel over control appears to be one of efficiency. It appears to be acceptable to attempt to control behaviour unsatisfactorily in an inefficient hit-or-miss fashion but it is not acceptable to determine the laws of learning and then to apply them to facilitate learning which is a precise, scientific means of control. Crichton quotes the American psychologist McConnel in the introduction to his novel. In trying to get this point across to his students he stressed that what we really must decide is the direction of the control.

Look, we can do these things. We can control behaviour. Now, who's going to decide what's to be done? If you don't get busy and tell me how I'm supposed to do it, I'll make up my own mind for you. And then it's too late.

49

Skinner, however, has already thought through the implications of his theories and how they might be applied in designing a culture.

The experimental analysis of behavior ... has a very special relevance to the design of cultures. Only through the active prosecution of such an analysis, and the courageous application of its results to daily life, will it be possible to design those contingencies of reinforcement which will generate and maintain the most subtle and complex behaviour of which men are capable.

(Skinner, 1966)

Over-population, overweight and war are, for Skinner, all results of man's sensitivity to reinforcement and thus can be dealt with by rearranging the reinforcement contingencies so that 'reinforcers which ordinarily generate unwanted behaviour simply do not do so'. He considers the contingencies of positive reinforcement arranged by present agencies such as governments and the church to be 'primitive'.

Economic reinforcement is badly programmed. Wage systems only rarely make effective use of positive reinforcement. . . . Education is still largely aversive; most students study mainly in order to avoid the consequences of not studying. In short some of the most powerful forces in human behaviour are not being effectively used. . . . Men are happy in an environment in which active, productive and creative behaviour is reinforced in effective ways.

Perhaps the best and certainly the most readable account of what a society based on theories of operant conditioning might be like is provided by Skinner in his novel *Walden Two*. Written in 1948, it outlines his modern Utopia and discusses the ethical problems engendered by a social system which, amongst other things, can find no place for religion, democracy or notions of personal freedom. He pursues this theme in a more scholarly way in *Beyond Freedom and Dignity*, published in 1971, but let us look at the more immediately provocative *Walden Two*. It has been described as 'an extremely interesting discourse on the possibilities of social organization' (*New Yorker*); 'alluring in a sinister way, and appalling too' (*New York Times*); and 'a slur upon a name, a corruption of an impulse ... such a triumph of mortmain or the dead hand, has not been envisaged since the days of Sparta' (*Life*).

In *Walden Two* the members work for 'labour-credits'. Frazier, the founder of Walden, explains:

Labour-credits are a sort of money. But they're not coins or bills – just entries in a ledger. All goods and services are free as you saw in the dining room this evening. Each of us pays for what he uses with twelve hundred labour-credits each year – say, four credits for each workday. We change the value according to the needs of the community.... All we ask is to make expenses, with a slight margin of safety; we adjust the value of the labour-credit accordingly. At present it's about one hour of work per credit....

A credit system also makes it possible to evaluate a job in terms of the willingness of the members to undertake it. After all, a man isn't doing more or less than his share because of the time he puts in; it's what he's doing that counts. So we simply assign different credit values to different kinds of work and adjust them from time to time to the basis of demand.

The set-up is run by a Board of Planners who 'make policies, review the work of the Managers, keep an eye on the state of the nation in general. They also have certain judicial functions....' The Managers are 'specialists in charge of the divisions and services of Walden Two', such as health, food, education, etc, who work up to their post and are definitely not elected, for 'Managers aren't horrific personages, but carefully trained and tested specialists. How could the members gauge their ability?'

Children are reared in a sort of Kibbutz-style system by experts on child care and behaviour. But 'What about mother love?' as Castle, a sceptic visiting Walden, asks. Frazier confirms that it is supplied in 'liberal doses. But we don't limit it to mothers. We go in for father love too – for everybody's love – community love if you wish. Our children are treated with affection by everyone – and thoughtful affection too, which isn't marred by temper due to overwork or careless handling due to ignorance.'

Emotional development is particularly carefully handled:

As to emotions – we aren't free of them all, nor should we like to be. But the meaner and more annoying – the emotions which breed unhappiness – are almost unknown here, like unhappiness itself. We don't need them any longer in our struggle for existence.... Sorrow and hate – and the high voltage excitement of anger, fear and rage – are out of proportion with the needs of modern life, and they're wasteful and dangerous.

Self control is shaped up by procedures such as the following:

We give each child a lollipop which has been dipped in powdered sugar so that a single touch of the tongue can be detected. We tell him he may eat the lollipop later in the day, provided it hasn't already been licked ... we don't punish. We never administer an unpleasantness in the hope of repressing or eliminating undesirable behaviour.

Education is, however, not only made easier by the application of scientific principles of learning but also by the fact that there is no contradiction between home and school.

The ordinary teacher spends a good share of her time changing the cultural and intellectual habits which the child acquires from its family and surrounding culture. Or else the teacher duplicates home training in a complete waste of time. Here we can almost say that the school is the family and vice versa.

These extracts are but brief glimpses into the workings of Walden and are meant to whet the appetite of the reader for the novel itself. *Walden Two* demonstrates the possible outcome if a learning theory explanation of behaviour were adopted and applied in practice. The reader is left to form his own judgement whether the explanation or its outcome are satisfactory.

3
Language and communication

The importance of language to man's civilization is universally acknowledged. Huxley, in his preface to *Brave New World Revisited*, expresses this powerfully if somewhat dogmatically:

Language has made possible man's transition from animality to civilization. Language permits its user to pay attention to things, persons and events, even when the things and persons are absent and the events are not taking place.

Moreover, it appears from the early work of anthropologists such as Sapir and Whorf that language may be the basis for our reality. This work, usually referred to as the 'linguistic relativity' hypothesis, demonstrates how the specific language we use constains our view of the world. Whorf (1956) summarizes this in the following way:

The world is ... a kaleidoscope flux of impressions which has to be organized by our minds – and this means largely by the linguistic systems in our minds. We cut nature up, organize it into concepts and ascribe significances as we do, largely because we are parties to an agreement to organize it in this way – an agreement that holds throughout our speech community and is codified in the patterns of our language. The agreement is, of course, an implicit and unstated one, *but its terms are absolutely obligatory* ... No individual is free to describe nature with absolute impartiality but is constrained to certain modes of interpretation even while he thinks himself most free.

The obvious implication of this is that people who speak

different languages live in different worlds. The way we structure our world is apparently governed by the terms in which we speak. An example of this is in the different ways different language users classify aspects of their experience. If they use one word for a set of objects then those objects are alike for them. Speakers of different languages, with several different words for subsets of these objects, will see them as being dissimilar. A few examples may illustrate this intriguing but difficult concept. In England, snow does not figure largely in our lives and so we make do with one word in English and very rarely distinguish between different types of snow. For Eskimos, however, snow is of central importance and consequently there are many different words to refer to specific types and uses of snow – newly fallen snow, hard snow, snow used for building, etc. Similarly, the Hopi Indians have only one word to refer to what appear to us to be different aspects of aviation such as pilot, fly, aeroplane, etc. Even more pertinently, our present society has necessitated the inclusion of many new words to express extremely subtle differences which not only non-industrialized peoples ignore but also many of the members of this society. The man in the street has no need for distinctions such as psychiatrist, psychologist, psychotherapist.

Orwell, in his *1984*, was also aware of this function of language. In 'Newspeak' words like 'freedom', 'peace' and 'liberty' were removed from the dictionaries and their use was banned. 'The purpose of Newspeak was not only to provide a medium of expression for the world view and mental habits proper to Ingsoc, but to make all other modes of thought impossible. ... Newspeak was designed not to extend but to *diminish* the range of thought. ...' This link between language and thinking has occupied a central position in both theory and research for many years. Although a lengthy discussion of this topic would not be appropriate here, it is perhaps worth mentioning the pioneering work of Piaget and Vygotsky in this area. Vygotsky's (1962) conclusions regarding the relationship of thought and language are expressed in his conviction that:

Thought is not merely expressed in words; it comes into existence through them.

We may say, then, that language is of supreme importance because it performs two major functions.

1 Language is necessary as a system of responses by which individuals can communicate, and
2 Language is necessary as a system of responses required for thinking.

This introduction to the importance of language is of necessity brief, as the field is both vast and complex and as such requires a full book in its own right, which will appear in this series (A6). Similarly, only a brief background overview will be given of how language is 'acquired'. The term 'acquire' is used advisedly in order to avoid begging the question as to whether language is innate or learned, a recent battleground in psychology and philosophy for the rationalist as against empiricist schools of thought (currently referred to as cognitivism and behaviourism respectively). The major protagonists are Chomsky, a rationalist, and Skinner, whose behaviourist theories we have already discussed. It is generally agreed that the child learns the language of those who socialize him but the way in which this learning occurs, and the extent to which learning is necessary, is still a current controversy which need not be elaborated here. Chomsky's theories are in the rationalist tradition and are founded on the central tenet that the basis of language is innate. Basically Chomsky maintains, for various reasons, that language is so complex that we cannot possibly just learn it from our environment but that we have an innate language acquisition device (L.A.D.) which consists of a grammar or system for understanding and producing a potentially infinite number of sentences.

Skinner views language as learned, verbal behaviour. McGrath (1970) has summed up this position in two sentences.

The words of others are stimuli that come to have meaning because they occur in association with rewarding or punishing circumstances. The utterances of the child are responses which become learned because they help (or hinder) his attempts to get what he wants.

Skinner believes that the production of language is achieved by a process of operant conditioning whereby an infant's successive approximation to recognizable words are reinforced by his parents. The work on operant verbal conditioning (discussed later) shows that verbal behaviour *can* be put under operant control but does not, of course, prove that this process is *neces-*

sary to language learning.

Many psychologists interested in language are coming to the conclusion that this controversy is somewhat academic and unrelated to language in the real world. Moreover, it appears that both approaches are relevant and are not mutually exclusive. Learning theorists tend to concentrate on the earliest aspects of speech development, whereas cognitive theorists tend to concern themselves with later, more complex language and the grammars which may account for it. Happily, at last, there appear to be attempts to meet half-way, whereby both learned and innate components of grammar are recognized. The role of imitation in language development is also becoming increasingly recognized.

This introduction, stressing the importance and complexity of language as an area of study, is meant to provide a background for the more social psychological aspects of language which we will consider in this chapter. We will look at language as a means of social control, the effect of social forces on language development and language as but one aspect of the wider notion of communication.

Social class and language

In spite of the popular myth regarding the breakdown of the class system in Britain, it has frequently been shown that indices of social class, e.g. occupation, are good predictors of many forms of social behaviour, especially communication skills. Although social class and language immediately makes one think of accent or dialect, Bernstein's concern has been in comparing the structure and use of working-class and middle-class language (Bernstein, 1971). It must be emphasized that Bernstein's claims refer to the 'lower working class' (unskilled and semi-skilled workers) compared with the 'middle class'. He maintains that the middle class and lower working class use language in different ways so that they are almost using different languages. Bernstein's basic distinction is between *'public'* and *'formal'* language. (He later replaced these terms by 'restricted code' and 'elaborated code' respectively.) Public language or restricted code is used virtually exclusively by the lower working class but is available for use by middle class to suit the occasion. Formal language or elaborated code is the form most often employed by the middle class.

As a sociologist, Bernstein maintains that

(a) the social structure of society (or class system) determines
(b) the nature of social relations between people which
(c) give rise to different linguistic codes.

The middle class and lower working class have different systems of social relations – the lower-working-class system is geared to the need to maintain rapport and solidarity, whereas the middle-class system is geared to the expression of individual differences and long-term goals. The result is two different linguistic codes. Bernstein (1961) defines these two codes in the following way:

A public language is a form of language use which can be marked off from other forms by the rigidity of its syntax and the restricted use of formal possibilities for verbal organization.

A formal language is one in which the formal possibilities and syntax are much less predictable for any one individual and the formal possibilities for sentence organization are used to clarify meaning and make it explicit.

He clarifies this distinction by the example of a middle-class and a lower-working-class mother on a bus with their respective children. The lower-working-class mother/child interaction takes the following form:

MOTHER: Hold on tight.
CHILD: Why?
MOTHER: Hold on tight.
CHILD: Why?
MOTHER: You'll fall.
CHILD: Why?
MOTHER: I told you to hold on tight, didn't I?

As Bernstein says, as the result of such an exchange 'the natural curiosity of the child has been blunted'. The mother's language is basically concerned with maintaining power rather than with the imparting of information. In the second example, involving the middle-class mother, the emphasis is on reason and cause and effect. It is a teaching rather than a power maintaining procedure.

MOTHER: Hold on tightly, darling.
CHILD: Why?
MOTHER: If you don't you will be thrown forward and you'll fall.

CHILD: Why?
MOTHER: Because if the bus suddenly stops you'll jerk forward on to the seat in front.
CHILD: Why?
MOTHER: Now darling, hold on tightly and don't make such a fuss.

Bernstein lists many factors distinguishing the two codes (see Robinson (1972) for a full list) but the major differences are probably the following:

1 Predictability – lower-working-class sentences are far more predictable after the first few words than middle-class sentences.
2 Vocabulary – in one study Bernstein found that apprentices were only slightly inferior to public schoolboys on Raven's Progressive Matrices (a non-verbal test of intellectual ability) but were greatly inferior on the Mill Hill Vocabulary Test.
3 Sentence Structure – the lower-working-class employ much shorter, grammatically simple sentences coupled with the repetitive use of conjunctions; also fewer subordinate clauses are used by lower-working-class speakers.
4 'Sympathetic Circularity' – the lower working class employ more phrases demanding reassurance like 'wouldn't it?' 'you see?' 'you know' 'know what I mean?' Compare this to the middle-class preference for the greater use of 'I'.

Bearing in mind these differences between elaborated and restricted code users in terms of the sort of language they model and the differential encouragement they give to the linguistic efforts of their children, we should expect vast differences in the language ability of middle- and lower-working-class children. Bernstein argues that this is the main reason why lower-working-class children experience difficulties 'in trying to cope with education as it is given in our schools'. Children who are thus linguistically deprived,

will experience difficulty in learning to read, in extending their vocabulary, and in learning to use a wide range of formal possibilities for the organization of verbal meaning; their reading and writing will be slow and will tend to be associated with a concrete, activity-dominated, content; their powers of verbal comprehension will be limited; grammar and syntax will pass them by; the propositions they use will suffer from a large measure of dislocation; their verbal planning function will be restricted; their thinking will tend to be rigid – the number of new relationships available to them will be very limited.

My own research (Wheldall, 1974) has shown very great differences in ability to comprehend different sentence structures between lower-working-class and middle-class children who are about to start infant school. Nursery school education, however, has a very beneficial effect on the receptive language development of lower-working-class children, bringing them up to the level of their middle-class peers.

Such findings on working-class children tend to contradict the rather glib claims of some language theorists who stress the rapidity of language acquisition as evidence for their theoretical perspective that the development of language is to a large degree innately determined and as evidence for an innate language acquisition device.

For example, Miller and McNeil (1969) maintain that,

By four years of age, he [the normal child] will have mastered the entire complex and abstract structure of English. In slightly less than two years, therefore, children acquire full knowledge of the grammatical system of their native tongue. This stunning intellectual achievement is routinely performed by every pre-school child.

The main reason for such extravagant claims being made is the preference, by such theorists, for the in-depth case study approach focusing on single children who are usually from a middle-class background. For example, Lois Bloom's influential research was carried out on only three children who were 'all first born children of families in which both parents were college graduates and native speakers of American English.... The Peabody Picture Vocabulary test, administered to each of the children at three years, produced mental age scores that ranged from 3 years 10 months to 5 years 8 months' (Bloom, 1970). It must be emphasized that middle-class children, especially of academic parents, probably acquire language in a very 'abnormal' way, i.e. in a way different from the majority of children. Firstly they are in a highly verbal environment and secondly the encouragement they get to be verbal is considerable. Moreover, such parents are also more likely to 'teach' aspects of grammar and to encourage the child to ask questions about language.

As Skinner (1971) says, 'The size of a child's vocabulary or

59

the grammatical forms he uses are not a function of development age but of the verbal contingencies which have prevailed in the community to which he has been exposed. ...' Unfortunately, the working-class child's community tends to be less than stimulating linguistically and to attach little importance to education. Morton and Goldman (1969) stress the importance of this consideration.

... children from lower-working-class homes are hampered by the home culture (of which economic poverty is part) and their teacher's failure to understand the culture. In contrast many middle-class infants have a wider vocabulary and reading ability fostered by their parents, and school socialization complements and reinforces their family socialization process.

Thus for many children of lower-working-class parents, the first day at infants school must be like entering a foreign country with strange customs such as reading, writing and painting, with strange objects like books and pictures and, perhaps even more frightening, a strange language, the elaborated code. Not only will the teacher use formal language or the elaborated code but the materials she uses, the story books and the reading books, will also be in this form. Similarly, the lifestyle depicted in many of these materials is middle-class orientated. The 'Ladybird' reading scheme features eminently reasonable mothers who are forever able to leave the nice house with a garden and take the children out in the car to the country. The middle-class lifestyle is presented as the norm and in middle-class language. It is not surprising, therefore, that the working-class child (who has not had nursery school education) does not 'take' to school, nor is it surprising that such children are highly prone to be rejected as 'failures' of the educational system.

Language and social influence

We have seen how different social structures identified by social class give rise to different forms of language or linguistic codes geared to the specific needs and values of the specific culture. This tends to perpetuate differences between classes and, it appears, may function to maintain the social order. On a less scientific level, this was demonstrated earlier in the fifties by the half-joking, half-serious concern with U and non-U speech. Nancy Mitford, popularizing the work of Alan Ross, turned social-class differences in language into a sort of parlour game. What started off as a sort of jokey dig at the working class became a bible for the rising petit-bourgeoisie who, anxious not to betray their class origins, hid behind a wall of snobbery. The most celebrated example is 'toilet', which was very non-U; to be U you referred to the lavatory or perhaps even better, the 'loo'. Similarly, a U person or an aspiring U person would always say napkin and never say serviette. Amazingly this is still going on. Ross now has a new book out entitled, predictably, *Don't Say It* (1973). This provides fascinating examples of the subtle ways in which language may be used to convey a little more than the manifest verbal content. Ross shows considerable insight into the nuances of one-upmanship as shown by the following examples.

bath – 'I'm just going to take a bath' is non-U. The U for it is 'I'm just going to have my bath'. The implication of the use of 'my' is that the U have more baths than the non-U; this used to be true and, astonishingly, still is. There are, however, some very dirty U people.

book – is the almost universal non-U word for magazine. The use would seem to imply that the non-U do not read many actual books but this may not be true.

tea – 'High tea' is a meal that the U think the non-U have. But the non-U, although they do have the meal that the U think they have, do not call it this; they just call it 'tea'. Hence the non-U if they wish to refer to what the U call tea, have to do so by some other name; and they do, for they call that meal 'afternoon tea'. So, perversely, the only people who actually use the expression 'high tea' are the U; they sometimes have it, too, and refer to it by this name, as, for instance, before going to the cinema.

Possibly my favourite example of how language may function to convey more than the surface form of the utterance is provided by Brown (1965):

The scene was a dinner party; the guests were all political scientists or people in the foreign service and they were all chiefly interested in the problems of newly independent nations. The conversation turned to Nigeria and a young specialist on economic development remarked: 'That's a place I've not been to'. A few seconds later a young political scientist said: 'I've not been there either and it isn't the only place I haven't been to'. The young

61

economist flushed, in his wife's hand the wine glass trembled, the hostess looked embarrassed.

Instead of saying, 'I have never been there', he chose to reverse it, thereby implying that he had been to lots of other places. This clumsy piece of boastful one-upmanship was smartly dealt with by the acute but perhaps unkind political scientist. Similarly, one of my friends recently ended a telephone conversation with 'Well, I hope I'll see you soon, John'. The reply was not 'Sure, see you soon' or 'It'd be great to see you' as expected, but the ominous 'You'll see me soon'. We puzzled over this for days; was it a threat or a promise? Or was it indicative of extreme egocentricism? We never quite decided but John was certainly made aware of his *faux pas* on our next meeting when we teased him unmercifully.

Thus it can be seen that by the very subtle use of words and the structure which we place on them, we can convey very discrete meanings and affect behaviour accordingly. Whether we refer to someone as thin or slim can have a considerable effect on that person depending on whether he, or more usually she, is under- or over-weight. Similarly, we may describe someone as calm, cool or cold, thereby expressing very subtle but different emotional evaluations of the person's conduct. We use syntax to stress the relevant aspects of our statements. One would not often say 'A car ran over my dog'; usually one would stress that it was 'my dog' and hence the passive, 'My dog was run over by a car'.

The following two sections describe two other powerful ways in which language controls and is itself controlled.

Address rules

A white policeman yelled, 'Hey, boy! Come here!' Somewhat bothered, I retorted: 'I'm no boy!' He then rushed at me, inflamed, and stood towering over me, snorting, 'What d'ja say, boy?' Quickly he frisked me and demanded, 'What's your name, boy?' Frightened, I replied, 'Dr Poussaint, I'm a physician.' He angrily chuckled and hissed, 'What's your first name, boy?' When I hesitated he assumed a threatening stance and clenched his fists. As my heart palpitated, I muttered in profound humiliation, 'Alvin'.   (Poussaint, 1971)

The power of language to demand or inflict status is clearly shown in this graphic example of Dr Poussaint's humiliation. To the white policeman, Dr Poussaint was an inferior Negro whatever his occupation and hence his constant use of the term 'boy' to a mature man.

Address rules, the laws governing how we refer to others, reflect and maintain differentials of status. They may also be said to define role relationships (a person's role in a situation is the sort of behaviour he habitually uses in that situation). Perhaps the clearest example of such a rule is the essential feature of many languages which demands differentiation in terms of grammar between the use of the two forms of 'you'. In French *tu* and *vous* distinguish much more than just singular or plural. *'Tutoyer'* and *'vousvoyer'* are verbs derived from these two forms which indicate the closeness of the speaker to the listener. *Tutoyer* not only means to address someone as *tu* or *toi* (instead of *vous*) but also to be on familiar terms with someone. *Vous* would always be used to a stranger or to someone whom one knows but slightly. It will also be used as a sign of respect by a younger person to an older unrelated person. Robinson (1972) argues that 'mutual T and mutual V came to mark equality, emphasizing either solidarity and familiarity (T) or unfamiliarity (V), while the asymmetrical use of V to a superior and T to inferior came to mark a difference in power'. French colonialists would *'tu-toi'* their slaves or servants in the same way as the white policeman used 'boy' to Dr Poussaint.

In English this distinction has disappeared (thou and ye) but we still, to a degree, operate fairly tight rules regarding proper names and titles. A junior employee would know better than to call the head of his firm by his first name on their first meeting and maybe on subsequent meetings. If he did not 'know better' his lapse of 'form' would quickly be made clear to him. We automatically call children by their first names even if we have only just met them but even the most liberal of us may be slightly shaken if the child refers to you immediately by your first name. It is a current fashion to say 'Oh, call me Frank' or 'Pinky' or 'G.T.' or whatever but the point remains that it is the privilege of the person of superior status to relax the rule. I still feel a little suspicious of the 'Call me Bob', all-boys-together routine which is becoming prevalent even on business footings. Am I a reactionary or is it paranoia? Perhaps I do not want to be lulled into a false sense of security.

The interpretation of these rules also functions as an indicator of other aspects of the speaker. The use of surnames between colleagues smacks of public school and Oxbridge. Similarly, the over-cautious mutually consistent use of Mr, Mrs and Miss (and now Ms?) is seen by some to be 'very lower-middle class' whereas consistent 'Sir' or Mr to arguable superiors is seen as working class. Non-academics often refer to professors as prof. – a term hardly ever used by academics. It seems that you have to know the rules to be allowed to flout or bend them. The use of these rules is also closely tied to the situation. A manager is unlikely to be pleased if his affectionate secretary calls him 'Bubbles' in front of clients, let alone in front of his wife! He will probably not mind, however, if the lady in the canteen calls him 'ducks' or 'luv' as it is accepted that these expressions of devotion are freely and universally given.

Operant verbal conditioning
In Chapter 2 on social learning we discussed how stimuli may be conditioned to become reinforcers by occurring simultaneously with unconditioned reinforcers such as food. We noted that both attention and approval are very powerful conditioned social reinforcers. Verbal expressions of approval in particular, such as 'Fine', 'Good boy', 'That's great' may be used successfully to shape up many forms of behaviour including verbal behaviour. Greenspoon (1955) showed how one could virtually control what a person said by the selective use of verbal signals of approval. This process is known as operant verbal conditioning.

In an early demonstration, Greenspoon asked two groups of subjects to emit words at random for fifty minutes. In the first group he reinforced emitted plural words by saying 'mm – hmm', signalling approval, and signalled disapproval, 'huh-uh', of singular words. In the second group he reversed the procedure. In both groups the emission of the reinforced word-type showed an increase whereas the emission of the alternative word-type decreased, extinguished by a form of punishment. This finding has been repeated many times, showing that one can condition a wide range of verbal behaviours by a variety of conditioned reinforcers. Non-verbal reinforcers such as head nods or smiles were found to work equally well.

People can apparently be thus conditioned to make more

statements about themselves simply be reinforcing any statement including the words 'I', 'we', 'myself', etc. A good interviewer will probably make use of this technique to draw out his
subject without perhaps realizing what he is doing. Again we
must remember that this is not an insidious subversive brain-
washing technique but a demonstration of the way in which
verbal behaviour is controlled in everyday life. We tell new-
comers to a job that they will soon fit in with the rest of the staff
but what actually often happens is that their behaviour is shaped
to fit in. If the staff behave in a cool, serious way towards each
other the newcomer's attempts at light relief will either be
ignored or punished by means of icy stares, or silences. More
desirable behaviour such as a hushed inquiry after a person's
health may not be reinforced by heavy back-slapping or even a
smile. The merest sign of acceptance will serve as a reinforcer
or alternatively the temporary cessation of social punishment –
i.e. negative reinforcement.

What is perhaps even more interesting is how our verbal behaviour changes under different conditions due to different reinforcement contingencies. When staying with old friends in London I find myself immediately slipping back into a version of
our old schoolboy humour, including bad impersonations, silly
voices, numerous changes of accent and frequent hysterical
bouts of laughter. Compare this to my verbal behaviour in the
academic world, which consists of a reasonably constant tone of
voice, indulging in occasional intellectual witticisms coupled
with polite smiles. This Jekyll and Hyde switch is not so bizarre
as it sounds. With my London friends, silly verbal behaviour is
reinforced; the heavy academic style is not, and may even be
punished by ridicule. Similarly, I would hardly be reinforced
for silly verbal behaviour when giving a paper to the British
Psychological Society. This illustrates the nature of discriminative stimuli perfectly – my London friends are the discriminative stimulus for my silly verbal behaviour as I have been reinforced for it in their presence in the past.

A more disturbing side to the operant verbal conditioning
research is that opinion statements may also be controlled in this
way – a factor which must be taken into account in public-
opinion polling. The F scale (described in Chapter 4) which
measures authoritarian attitudes was filled in by a number of
subjects under varying reinforcement conditions. Singer (1961)

found that by saying 'good' or 'right' following every pro-democratic, anti-authoritarian statement endorsed by a subject, he could increase the total number of pro-democratic responses made. This sort of experiment also demonstrates how the experimenter effects reported by Rosenthal (see Chapter 1) could arise, i.e. subjects may easily be conditioned into responding as the experimenter wishes without possibly even the experimenter realizing what is happening.

Non-verbal communication

Winston kept his back to the telescreen. It was safer, though, as he well knew, even a back can be revealing. ...
His face remained completely inscrutable. Never show dismay! Never show resentment! A single flicker of the eyes could give you away. ...
His mocking eyes roved over Winston's face. 'I know you', the eyes seemed to say 'I see through you, I know very well why you didn't go to see those prisoners hanged.'

These extracts from Orwell's *1984* describe a form of communication which we all indulge in and understand to a greater or lesser degree. I'm referring to communication without words, non-verbal communication or, as it is sometimes popularly called, 'body language'. A book of this very name (Fast, 1971) was recently published to make us all aware of what our bodies are signalling to each other. According to the cover 'blurb', 'The body language of lapel-grabbers, backslappers, and heavy breathers is apparent to everyone, but are you hip to the leg-crossing lingo, which can signal sexual refusal? Do you get the message when a woman nonchalantly flipping her curls, flashes the palm of her hand to you? ... studies have shown that body language can often contradict the spoken language. It's a lot like the old song about "your lips tell me no-no, but there's yes-yes in your eyes ...".'

There is, however, thankfully a more serious side to this rampant sexism; recent research really is identifying and investigating many aspects of communication of which we are largely unconscious.

The processes and mechanisms by which we try to 'follow' what another person is saying involve a guessing strategy in which we combine what cues we can get from the speaker with our pre-existing expectations of what we think he is going to say. Furthermore, we supplement linguistic cues with visual and situational prompts, such as the speaker's facial expression, amount of eye-contact, use of gesture, tone of voice, use of physical contact, stance and use of distance. Current research, by social psychologists such as Argyle, has revealed the underlying importance of non-verbal communication. It may serve the purpose of elucidating, emphasizing, neutralizing, negating or otherwise altering that which a person states manifestly. On occasions, it may even replace verbal utterances altogether.

As Polhemus (1973) says,

The body has an iconography of signs and symbols. The clothes we put on and how we wear them, the ornaments we hang on ourselves, the expressions we put on our faces, the gestures we use, even the way we walk – all these are symbols to the rest of the world (or at least to the rest of our own society). They project our 'body image'.

Earlier in this chapter we commented on the way language is influenced by social forces and in turn acts as social influence. We referred specifically to the way in which slight changes of synonyms or word order can sometimes affect the meaning. This effect is intensified by the use of non-verbal cues in addition. Perhaps we should also stress the point that context is a very important determinant of how a message will be received. Context, the time and place and situation, generates expectancies of what we think a person will say. Each person's individual context will also be influenced by his feelings at a particular time. If one is feeling rather paranoid it is possible to take 'nice day' as a sarcastic remark. Similarly, different people may perceive the same manifest context differently. In an interview, the interviewer may feel at ease and make a joke which the interviewee may attempt to reply to seriously. Non-verbal cues should help to facilitate such situations. We normally signal by our facial expressions or tone of voice that we are making a joke.

Argyle (1972) identifies three principal roles of non-verbal communication (N.V.C.). The first is the communication of interpersonal attitudes and emotions.

He argues that the communication of affect or emotion is more reliably conveyed by non-verbal cues and that we tend to believe such cues more than verbal signals. Secondly, N.V.C. may be used to support verbal communication, by providing a sort of punctuation to our utterances by means of voice features and other cues. He quotes Abercrombie as saying 'We speak with our vocal organs but converse with our whole body'. Thus we may complete the meaning of utterances by pointing or gesturing and we can synchronize our verbal interactions by cuing each other by means of head-nods and eye-gaze when we stop and start talking. N.V.C. also tells us if the other person is bored or not understanding, usually by posture and facial expression, and we can in turn signal our attentiveness to a speaker by nodding, smiling, etc. Argyle's third role for N.V.C. is to replace speech when speech becomes impossible. The deaf sign languages are obvious examples of this, as are the gestures of tic-tac men at a race course or the gesture languages that sometimes develop in noisy factories. Even more interesting, from the psychological point of view, is the fact that at last we appear to be breaking through the man/animal language barrier by means of this third role of N.V.C. Previous attempts to teach chimpanzees to talk have all failed, presumably due to articulation problems engendered by the chimp's different vocal organs. A recognition of these production problems led Gardner and Gardner to teach their chimp Washoe to communicate using the American Sign Language. Similarly, Premack taught Sarah, another chimpanzee, to communicate by means of plastic coloured shapes which signify words. Both Washoe and Sarah have demonstrated their ability both to comprehend language in these terms and also to produce meaningful sentences which they had not previously been taught.

The forms of N.V.C. are many and various. The main types of non-verbal cues are summarized below, working, in a sense, outwards, from the manifest verbal utterance to the wider aspects.

Voice features

This area is often referred to as *paralinguistics* and includes accent, voice quality, intonation, etc. It's a case of 'It's not what you say, it's the way that you say it.' We use intonation to punctuate our sentences and sometimes to alter the effective grammar. We can make a statement into a question by adopting a rising intonation – 'You are going to the cinema tonight?' Apparently Malcolm X, addressing an audience of white liberals, used this to very dramatic effect by proclaiming the same accusatory statement four times, moving the stress successively one place each time.

What have you done?
What *have* you done?
What have *you* done?
What have you *done*?

We can also convey by means of voice features very different emotional meanings to our utterances. 'The King is dead' pronounced by a mourning queen and a jubilant revolutionary are likely to be immediately, recognizably different. Speech errors also provide extra information. Repetitions and stutters are indicative of anxiety, whereas 'ahs and ers' are used to create time to think whilst signalling that one wishes to continue speaking.

Facial cues
This refers to the use of facial expression, head-nods and eye-movements. As we have seen, head-nods can be very powerful reinforcers. Also, we can sychronize our verbal interactions by signalling, 'I agree-carry on' with one nod or, by giving several quick nods, say 'I want to speak now.'

Facial expressions are used basically to convey emotion. We can all recognize the six basic facial expressions identified by Schlosberg (1952): happiness; surprise; fear; anger; disgust; contempt. Apparently our ability to differentiate between them, however, decreases the 'closer' they are to each other in terms of the Schlosberg circle. This consists of the six emotions detailed above following each other on the circle in the above order in terms of similarity, with the last item, contempt, being close to happiness. The differences are basically conveyed by means of changes in three areas of the face: the mouth, the eyes and the brows.

The eyes have long been known as the 'mirror of the soul'. We speak of the 'evil eye' and the 'dirty look'. Argyle has made a particular study of gaze which can convey a variety of meanings dependent upon the context and the facial expression of the one who's gazing. A gaze can thus be amorous, aggressive, friendly or just curious. By altering the length and the overtness of the gaze we can indulge in flirtatious eye-play. Again eye-contact is also used to regulate verbal exchanges.

Gestural and postural cues

Body Language, the book previously referred to, set out to teach the meanings of postural cues concentrating heavily on providing tips for the sexual athlete. Postural cues may convey sexual attitudes but one suspects that much that is read into postural behaviour may be just wishful thinking. Posture can also convey aggression and dominance. Similarly, posture can also be a good indicator of social class. Girls of different social classes both wearing clothes from 'Bus Stop' may, according to my bachelor friends, be socially identified by means of posture. The middle-class girl will have a more erect posture compared with the more round shouldered posture preferred by many working-class girls.

Gesture refers to the use of movements by the hands in particular but also other parts of the body to convey messages. We point to make our meaning clear or make a rude sign to show disapproval. We also make use of heavily stereotyped gestures which have very specific meanings. Such gestures are known as *emblems* and include the clenched fist to symbolize anger or drawing the hand across the brow to indicate fatigue. In a more extreme form we end up with the sign language used by the deaf. The scientific study of posture and gesture is known as *kinesics*.

Proximity and touch

Bodily contact is something of a taboo in Western culture. A few years ago in an article in the *Guardian*, Gillian Tindall reflected on the 'touch phobia' in operation in this otherwise permissive society. Miss Tindall examined some of the effects this taboo has on everyday life, especially for those who 'have no-one left whom they can legitimately cuddle', i.e. the widowed, childless, unmarried or otherwise unattached. She quoted the typically effusive foreigner as at least being less inhibited in terms of person-to-person contact than the supremely reticent British. All this is due, she concluded, to a pathological sex sensitivity inherent in modern British and American culture, so that 'We have reached the state in which we cannot readily touch a member of the opposite sex because we feel that would lead to sexual intercourse, and we cannot touch a member of our own sex because it mustn't lead to sexual intercourse'.

Everyday experience suggests that Miss Tindall is absolutely right. Walking down Oxford Street, confronting a surging mass of bodies, it seems likely that one must experience contact with a large number of them. But, due to the swervings and weavings which we all perform in a vast lobster quadrille, the number of persons we actually touch is remarkably small and each of these encounters must immediately be followed by apology. Failure to abide by this implicit code results in social sanction, commonly taking the form of a glare and/or profuse 'tutting' which, roughly translated, means: 'someone has invaded my personal space' or 'I have been sexually molested'. Jourard has charted the touch permissiveness of American students and has found very great differences in who is touched by whom and where on the body.

Similarly, Westerners are also very sensitive to the proximity of other persons. Perhaps we do not want others to get too close in case they might touch us. It has been found that the permitted degree of closeness varies greatly across cultures, a factor of which diplomats must be especially aware. When using a communal urinal a gentleman must always use the next but one space available. To use a neighbouring space, when not absolutely vital, would suggest to the affronted first-comer that one had 'gay' intentions.

Proxemics, 'the use of social and personal space and man's perception of it' as defined by Hall (1963) is a theory which is mainly applicable in the U.K. and U.S.A. It postulates allowable degrees of proximity according to the intimacy of the relationship. Thus, minimal distance is permissible in a committed intimate relationship, but on a business level, seven to twelve feet is usual; your bank manager will keep his distance and hence his neutrality with the aid of a wide desk. Argyle argues that distance is not the only factor in that its effect can be dramatically altered by eye-gaze. Hence an intimate distance can be drastically reduced by avoidance of eye-gaze (as in a crowded tube train), in contrast with the heightened intimacy of a long mutual gaze across a crowded room.

Argyle also argues that orientation is an important aspect of proxemics. Different seating positions are appropriate for different purposes. Sitting opposite is appropriate for competing or selling whereas sitting side by side is more appropriate for co-operating in some way. Height may also be important as height implies dominance. A high chair behind a large desk coupled

71

with a low guest's chair gives you both dominance and distance.

These are the main sources of N.V.C. A case can also be made for appearance, which is usually under direct conscious control in order to present the desired 'body image'. The city gent and the hippie are both striving to communicate 'look, I am this sort of person'. Badges, bowlers, tattoos, ear-rings, make-up, hair style, etc., are all used to get across this message. There are other 'possibilities' which we might include under N.V.C. For example, smell, which we take great pains to eliminate or disguise in order not to communicate the fact that we perspire. Smell is a very important form of communication in the animal kingdom and recent research on pheromones suggests that we may be much more susceptible to smell than we realize. For example, a study carried out amongst American college girls sharing the same dormitory found that over time their menstrual cycles, which were initially disparate, tended to coincide. This was explained in terms of the action of pheromones, chemical messengers communicating via the sense of smell. We also re-cognize and assign meanings to other physiological processes, such as wet palms – indicating anxiety – or heavy breathing – which suggests that the person is asthmatic or has been running or, on the telephone, has dubious intentions. E.S.P. may be an-other non-verbal means by which we communicate unknow-ingly. The considerable body of scientific research into para-psychology, coupled with the recent amazing demonstrations by Uri Geller, must have shaken the scepticism of many of us. But if telepathy does exist it is certainly beyond our powers to con-trol it at present.

Barriers to communication

Parry (1967) has approached the study of human communica-tion in a novel way by tabulating the ways in which communi-cation can fail. His concern is to identify what he considers to be the seven main barriers to communication. He does not claim that this list is exhaustive but argues rather that it provides a springboard for further study. His seven barriers do, however, account for many instances of breakdowns in communication, as we shall see.

(1) Limitation of the receiver's capacity

This refers to situations where the information presented may be sensible and logical but is presented at too great a rate or in too great a quantity for the receiver to 'take it in'. An obvious example is of a lecturer giving too much information too quickly. In preparing and delivering his lecture he must take into account the limitations of his audience, their age, their intelligence and level of sophistication with regard to the topic of the lecture. My own students will vouch for the fact that I initially experienced considerable difficulty in finding the right level at which to expound on my 'pet' topics in what were supposed to be introductory lectures.

(2) *Distraction*
Distraction refers to extraneous factors which interfere with the reception of messages, of which there are four main types. The first is the *competing stimulus* whereby reception is hindered by the presence of extra unwanted stimulation of the same sense. An example of this is when one tries to talk to someone when the television set is on – their eyes (and ears) tend to drift from you to the T.V. set. This is made much worse when the competing stimulus is very similar to the message being conveyed. It's bad enough trying to hold a conversation at a party at the best of times but when the group next to you is holding a similar conversation on the same topic it becomes chaotic.

Environmental stress also acts as a distractor. Extremes of temperature, humidity, ventilation, vibration, noise and glare all greatly affect one's ability to attend to a message. Similarly, *internal stress* such as anxiety, the effects of drugs or alcohol or ill health, all make concentration difficult.

Ignorance of the communicating medium can be such a distraction as to make communication almost totally impossible. If there is no common medium of communication available, communication cannot take place. One is unlikely to learn much studying at the Sorbonne if one cannot understand French.

(3) *The unstated assumption*
This is a very common form of misunderstanding whereby the speaker makes a concealed assumption over, for example, the meaning of a word or concept. This is particularly true of psychology where everyday words are taken over and given highly specific scientific meanings. In my introductory lectures I happily slipped into the jargon of learning theory, talking of rein-

73

forcement here and operants there, not to mention discriminative stimuli. No wonder my students collapsed with laughter at my lecture on barriers to communication!

(4) Incompatibility of schemas

Parry cites Vernon's definition of schemas as 'persistent, deep-rooted and well-organized classifications of ways of perceiving, thinking and behaving'. People with radically different schemas will assimilate and interpret data in different ways. Schemas may be termed incompatible when they present irreconcilable accounts of the same data. So we can expect little real communication to take place between say a socialist and a Tory talking about unemployment or between an atheist and a devout Christian debating the origins of the universe. Similarly within psychology; only recently have behaviourists and cognitivists considered it worthwhile to talk to each other. It remains to be seen how much real communication will occur.

(5) The influence of unconscious and partly conscious mechanisms

This refers to the barrier caused by expectations and prejudices regarding the other person at various levels of conscious control. If one suspects the motives of another person or if one feels uneasy in his presence, communication will be hindered. Sometimes we take an instant dislike to someone and find ourselves totally unsympathetic to his arguments. Often we realize later that this is because he reminds us of someone we do dislike and do disbelieve – an example of stimulus generalization. Freudians would argue that the phemonenon of projection is an example of this sort of barrier whereby a person interprets the behaviour of the other in terms of his own unconscious needs and impulses. His reception of the message is likely to be slanted in accordance with his private desires and fears. Parry also mentions social taboos as factors which prevent one from speaking one's mind. Sex, the social taboo of previous generations, has probably now been taken over by death insofar as people tend to be very reluctant to discuss it.

(6) Confused presentation

An obvious hindrance to successful communication as it reduces efficiency is confused presentation. No matter how interesting the topic, the message can easily fail if it is badly presented. Similarly a potentially dull or, on later reflection, a dubious argument may be eagerly absorbed if it is presented in a clear and preferably entertaining style. I am sure that my own early preference for Freudian psychology, which I later discarded, was due to the enthusiasm and professional delivery of my lecturers in that field. It is perhaps not politic to speculate why I was not turned on to learning theory earlier! Among the faults of a bad confused communicator are poor choice of words, rambling and failing to keep to the point, faulty emphasis and an unfortunate delivery. Other examples include the incomprehensible officialese on tax forms, welfare benefit forms and letters from solicitors.

(7) *Absence of communication channels*
This barrier may seem too obvious to include – the absence of any means of bringing potential sender and receiver into contact obviously means that no communication can take place. However, the importance of this barrier lies in the fact that sometimes an existing channel is more apparent than real. An announcement of war presented only on a V.H.F. radio station would inform very few of the populace of the national state of affairs. Similarly, few people would receive messages conveyed in the University Calendar. Old soldiers know only too well that the commanding officer's 'Any complaints?' is certainly a more apparent than real offer of a communication channel. Similarly, all too often the lecturer's 'Any questions?' at the end of a lecture functions merely as a signal to dash for the exit.

Thus we can see that communication is a very chancy business. Not only are there barriers as outlined above but all the possible misunderstandings induced by inappropriate or contradictory non-verbal cues, not to mention the involuntary flouting of address rules. Given also the heavy effect of social factors on language development it is a small miracle that some of us ever communicate successfully at all! What must become obvious, however, is why social psychologists are so fascinated by the topic of communication – with so much that can go wrong it is wide open for research, the relevance of which is both obvious and immediate.

4
Attitudes and prejudice

One of the silliest jokes I know concerns a city gent whose
bowler has been eaten by a farmer's goat. The farmer is less
than apologetic, causing the affronted gent to exclaim pomp-
ously, 'I don't like your attitude!' The farmer, not in the least
bit impressed, deflates him with the withering reply, 'Oh no, it
were your 'at 'e chewed ...'

Attitude is one of the many words which psychologists have
taken from common parlance and have redefined. This practice
tends to make the layman think he knows what the psychologist
is talking about when in fact the psychologist is probably talking
about something rather different. All of which makes the psychologist feel superior and the layman feel confused if not
downright cheated. What, then, do psychologists mean by the
term 'attitude'? And why are social psychologists so interested
in attitudes?

In our example above, the city gent is complaining that the
farmer is not treating him with the respect, if not the deference,
he thinks he deserves. The farmer's manner towards him suggests that he does not hold city types in high regard. He probably has in fact a *negative attitude* towards city gents.

As we have seen in the previous chapter, we often communicate our feelings about others by means of non-verbal cues. This
is particularly interesting in this context as the word attitude
used to refer to the way a person stands, i.e. his posture. The
Shorter Oxford English Dictionary defines attitude initially as

'a posture of the body proper to or implying some action or mental state'.

The meaning more relevant to our purposes here, however, is the second entry in the dictionary: 'settled behaviour or manner of acting, as representative of feeling or opinion' and hence 'attitude of mind: habitual mode of regarding anything'. Thus if we say we enjoy going to the cinema, greatly appreciate modern art and strongly support the Liberal party, we can be said to have positive attitudes towards the cinema, modern art and the Liberal party. Conversely, if we say we detest Chinese food, find football totally dull and protest about fluoridation of the water supply, we can be said to have negative attitudes towards these. We have attitudes towards specific objects which may be people, institutions, ideas, social issues, physical objects and so on. Not every individual has an attitude towards every possible object, however. Some potential objects of attitudes are not known to everybody. An African bushman will probably not have attitudes towards the atomic bomb or Vietnam as he has probably heard of neither. Similarly, some objects are subjectively too insignificant for everyone to have an attitude concerning them. A Glaswegian will probably not have an attitude towards the new one-way traffic system in Derby, even if he has heard of it. Similarly relatively few people will have attitudes towards existentialism, Schoenberg, the 'penny black', or the Guru Mahara'Ji.

The study of attitudes is central to social psychology; in fact it used to be considered so important that social psychology was once defined as 'the scientific study of attitudes'. Allport, one of the earliest and most important contributors to the theory of attitudes, was still convinced, in 1954, that 'the concept of attitude is probably the most distinctive and indispensable concept in contemporary, American social psychology. No other term appears more frequently in experimental and theoretical literature.' Today, social psychologists have wider interests (e.g. the study of groups and of language and communication) but there is still considerable interest and research into the various aspects of attitudes.

Before attempting to define and describe the term attitude as it is currently used, another brief look into the history of social psychology is necessary. This reveals that attitude is the latest concept in a series of supposed basic units of social analysis which have been proposed. McDougall (1908), who, as we have already noted, wrote one of the first books on social psychology, laid great store by the concept of *instinct* – 'the innate tendencies of thought and action that constitute the native basis of mind'.

Instincts were conceived of as innate predispositions to behave in a certain way. Each human being was said to be equipped with the same basic set of instincts which were, however, distributed in differing degrees of intensity. McDougall suggested the existence of five basic instincts: flight, repulsion, curiosity, self-abasement/self-assertion and the parental instinct. There were also rules of combination by which instincts combined in different ways to form propensities which in turn could combine to form sentiments which were persistent ways of orienting towards a given class of objects or ideas. The theory of instincts dominated social psychology for many years but this approach was limited by several major problems. Instinct theorists could not agree upon the number and nature of the basic instincts or even how to determine them. The same applied to propensities and sentiments and the rules of combination. Above all, they could not definitely prove the existence of these innate behavioural tendencies and tended to over-indulge themselves in creating new ones – a new instinct was 'discovered' to cover each new behaviour observed. From McDougall's basic five, the list of instincts postulated had grown to 15,000 by 1924!

With a rise of behaviourism in the decades following the 1920s, the concept of instinct was replaced by that of *habit* as the new unit of analysis. A habit was defined as a learned stimulus response bond which resulted in automatic responses given the appropriate stimulus conditions. Watson and others attempted to account for more complex behaviour in terms of combinations of simple learned habits and hence came face to face with very similar problems to those encountered by the instinct theorists. Since those early days of behaviourism, however, learning theory has advanced considerably so that 'habits' or similar concepts are still in evidence, albeit in more sophisticated theoretical paradigms of conditioning. The innate versus learned aspects of attitudes will be discussed further in the section on the acquisition of attitudes.

Following the demise of instincts and habits, a third unit of analysis was proposed, the *attitude*, which combines features from both of the two preceding concepts. Attitudes are *learned*, unlike instincts, and consist of *predispositions* to respond to a given object or class of objects rather than fixed responses like habits. It should perhaps be mentioned, however, in fairness to McDougall, that he did acknowledge that learning played a part in stabilizing and diversifying the instinctual response.

Attitudes are characterized by the fact that they persist over time as an orientation (either positive or negative) towards an object, or set of objects, about which people tend to disagree in their judgements. Rokeach (1965), a leading authority in the study of attitudes, has defined the term in the following way:

An attitude is a relatively enduring organization of beliefs around an object or situation predisposing one to respond in some preferential manner.

Hence a negative attitude towards coloured people consists of a person's collection of 'facts' about coloured people which may cause him to feel antipathy towards them resulting in him making this manifest either verbally or in how he acts towards coloured people. From this we can see that an attitude may be considered as being composed of three parts.

First, there is the person's knowledge about the object of the attitude; in the present example it consists of what he knows about coloured people. This may be a very biased collection of 'facts' which may not even have been acquired from first-hand experience. People who have never met persons of a particular race or group may well be convinced that Irishmen are stupid, or that Pakistanis smell, or that hippies are dirty, or that West Indians are only interested in sex and loud music. They will form such impressions on the basis of gossip, newspaper articles, T.V. programmes, etc., but may also have experienced the object of the attitude directly. When many people share the same view regarding the object of an attitude, for example students, and it is characterized by over-simplicity and superficial evidence, then this notion is known as a stereotype. A popular stereotype shared by people who dislike students is that they are all dirty, loud-mouthed, Communist know-alls who spend more time demonstrating than studying.

A person's knowledge of the 'facts' about the object of an attitude is referred to as the *cognitive* component. The word cognitive refers to the process of thinking and hence this component reflects the person's intellectual evaluation of the object. Some psychologists prefer to refer to this aspect as *belief*.

Secondly there is the affective component. As we have already noted, affect refers to emotions and feelings. So now we are talking not of what a person thinks about an object but of what he feels about it. If a person believes that hippies are sexually promiscuous and if he disapproves of sexual promiscuity, then he might well decide that he dislikes hippies. Previously we were concerned with judgements of belief, whether a thing was bad or good, true or false, etc., now we are concerned with like or dislike, approval or disapproval. These affective judgements are greatly influenced by a person's values – his beliefs about how a person ought and ought not to behave.

As Rokeach (1965) has suggested:

A grown person probably has tens of thousands of beliefs, hundreds of attitudes, but only dozens of values. A value system is an hierarchical organization – a rank ordering – of ideals or values in terms of importance. To one person truth, beauty and freedom may be at the top of the list, and thrift, order and cleanliness at the bottom: to another person, the order may be reversed.

In a sense these values may be regarded as abstractions or generalizations, as these general orientations will influence specific attitudes. A person who values freedom may well have favourable attitudes to the more specific freedom to strike or to demonstrate.

The third part of an attitude is often referred to as the *behavioural* component. This is concerned not with what a person believes or feels but with what he tends to do, how he behaves towards the object. This behaviour may be verbal or non-verbal. A skinhead might say he hates Pakistanis or actually involve himself in 'Paki-bashing'. It is a common finding, however, that what people say and what they actually do often differs greatly.

So now we may say that an attitude consists of

(a) What we know about an object
(b) How we feel about it
(c) What we tend to do about it.

It has been argued by some that a behavioural component is not essential. It does not always appear to be present, as in the case of a person who says that he likes opera but who never goes to see a performance nor ever listens to opera on record. In answer to this, Rokeach claims that there must have been a behavioural component at some time. The person must have heard opera on the radio once by accident or have heard records at a friend's house and must have remarked that he liked it. There must have been a behaviour from which the person inferred his attitude. This rather dogmatic position, however, omits any present behaviour from the attitude, i.e. what he tends to do about the object of the attitude now, except for verbal behaviour. Opinion refers to the verbal expression of a belief, value or attitude and is chiefly characterized by the fact that it must not be taken at face value. When questioned about his attitudes to various social issues a person may well not want to reveal to others or even to himself his real feelings. He may decide that it would not be politic to express his real views in support of anti-immigration policies and a desire to see hanging restored at a party given by Hampstead liberals. Consequently we can say that an opinion is a public expression of attitude as distinct from a private attitude which may be a more realistic reflection but which will only be expressed in conditions of privacy or trust.

A similar problem with this tripartite view of attitude lies in the fact that the three components do not always coincide. It is possible to like something which one knows is bad and feel antipathy towards something good. We often hear people say something like: 'Technically his voice is very good but I just can't bear Frank Sinatra' or 'He has a terrible reputation but I can't help liking him'. In this case the person's behaviour will be determined by the relative strengths of the evaluative and affective components and he will either switch off or sit back and enjoy Frank Sinatra on the television.

Similarly, it must be stressed that specific behaviours will be influenced by various attitudes and the context or situational conditions. Attitudes are predispositions to respond in a certain way, not fixed responses and hence they might or might not lead to a certain behaviour. We have already discussed how the cognitive or evaluative component and the affective component can be at odds and also how the situation can affect opinions as expressions of attitude. We should bear all of this in mind when considering the following example which illustrates that what people say and what they actually do can be very different.

In a now classic study conducted in 1934, La Pierre visited restaurants and hotels in the U.S.A. He was always accompanied by two Chinese companions and was only once refused service in spite of considerable anti-Chinese feeling in the U.S.A. at that time. However, when he subsequently wrote to the various establishments he had visited asking 'Will you accept members of the Chinese race as guests in your establishment?', over 90 per cent of the replies indicated that they would not. This demonstrates clearly what is commonly called attitude behaviour inconsistency. The inconsistency, however, is not so difficult to understand if we take into consideration the other attitudes of the hotel/restaurant managers. These will include attitudes towards good business practice; a 'scene' is not good for business. In addition to this, of course, is the fact that the manager may not have a very strong negative attitude towards Chinese people so that if he can avoid them he will but he will not put himself out to enforce this by physically ejecting them. Yet another factor is the public/private distinction. He may genuinely feel antipathy towards Chinese people and even be prepared to express it in the comparative anonymity of a letter but, if he feels that his attitude is not socially acceptable, he will be reluctant to express it in a crowded restaurant.

A further point which must be stressed concerning attitudes is their specificity. One cannot sensibly talk about an aggressive attitude (other than in the posture sense) since an attitude must necessarily specify the object. We can talk of positive attitudes towards Wagner, hanging and dogs, for example, or of negative attitudes towards Ford Cortinas, garlic and Picasso. It can thus be seen that attitudes are distinct from personality. Aggressive behaviour might well constitute part of a person's personality and this may be reflected in the behavioural component of some of his negative attitudes but it must be emphasized that attitudes necessarily specify an object.

A similar relationship exists between the concepts of attitude and culture. A culture consists of a set of beliefs and values which are so deeply rooted in the traditions of a race or creed or other enduring collective of persons that they exist irrespective of the individual differences between the members. This being so, it would be rather irrelevant to claim that a devout catholic whom you know has a negative attitude towards meat and a positive attitude towards fish every Friday! However, cultures can and do influence a person's attitudes in areas not specified by the culture. An example of this might be the influence of the protestant ethic on the rise of capitalism. Rokeach (1965) refers to faith as 'one or more beliefs a person accepts as true, good or desirable, regardless of social consensus or objective evidence, which are perceived as irrelevant'. He contrasts this with delusion – 'a belief held on faith judged by an external observer to have no objective basis and which is, in fact, wrong'.

In using the concept of attitude as a means of estimating a person's potential behaviour, however, we need to know more about the nature of his attitudes. This will involve attempts at accurate attitude measurement (discussed later). It is not sufficient to know that A has a positive attitude towards Wagner and that B has a negative attitude towards the 'pill'. C and D may have the same manifest attitudes respectively as A and B but there may be several dimensions on which they differ in respect to those attitudes.

Firstly, there is the obvious factor of *extremeness* – just how positive is A's attitude and how negative is B's? A may well like Wagner very much, but not so much as he likes Beethoven or Brahms and much more than Sibelius or Tchaikovsky. B may disapprove of contraception but be violently opposed to abortion.

Secondly, there is *cognitive content* which refers to the fact that people may have the same attitude but for different reasons. A may appreciate the structure of Wagner's operas, his idiosyncratic use of the *leitmotif* for communicating different moods, situations and characters. On the other hand, C may enjoy the stirring, powerful overtures. Similarly, B's attitude to the pill may be determined by his religious faith whereas D, an atheistic scientist, is concerned about the side-effects of the long-term use of oral contraceptives.

Differentiation is closely connected with cognitive content. It refers to the sophistication of a person's attitude – how clear and structured it is. In our examples, A may have studied Wagner for many years, discovering and considering his relative musical assets and deficits which has finally resulted in a critical but positive attitude to Wagner. B on the other hand may never even have considered the philosophical, psychological or physiological aspects of oral contraception but in that he perceives it as unnatural, his conclusion is that he is opposed to it.

A further consideration in evaluating attitudes is the degree to which a specific attitude is related to and integrated with other attitudes. This is referred to as *isolation*. Does the attitude exist in isolation from the person's other attitudes or is it closely bound up with a person's more general view? If B is a strict vegetarian, his attitude to the pill may form part of a complex of inter-related attitudes with the common theme of favouring folk medicine in preference to 'unnatural chemicals'. A's appreciation of Wagner may be totally unrelated to his other attitudes so that he may prefer to go to Italy rather than Germany for his holidays and sympathize more strongly with Sartre than Nietzche in his philosophy.

Finally, there is the *strength* of attitudes to be considered. If a person has held an extreme view for a long period of time in the face of opposing evidence, it is characterized as a strong attitude. A weak attitude would be susceptible to change with relative ease. Strength is related to extremeness but not exclusively, for we have all encountered individuals who have thrown everything into a sudden passion or conviction only to change to a view often diametrically opposed. M.P.s occasionally change their allegiance to the opposing political party. Our Wagner lover's strong attitude is not only extreme but has endured and is carefully worked out in terms of cognitive content and differentiation. If it is also integrated with his other attitudes, his personality, and with the attitudes of a group to which he belongs, it will be held even more strongly and hence will be even more resistant to change.

Why do we need attitudes?

Attitudes form a means by which we can structure our world, our experience. In order to cope with the continual influx of new information provided by our senses, we need some means of ordering and classifying that information. We need to know what to accept and what to reject, what to believe and what not to believe. Attitudes act as a sort of sieve or filter which cuts down the amount of new information we are faced with and allows us to relate new information to the information we already possess.

Try to imagine what it would be like to have to evaluate every new piece of information in isolation without yardsticks by which to decide its truth, meaningfulness, applicability, desirability, etc. One way of imagining this is to think back to an occasion when you confronted an idea or problem for the first time, about which you had no specific pre-formed attitudes. As an example we could take attitudes to modern art. Perhaps you encountered examples of Picasso's work in adolescence and did not know what to make of it. Perhaps you discussed it with your parents who dismissed it as rubbish. Your art teacher might have been very enthusiastic about Picasso's work, whereas a paperback history of art might have acknowledged his creativity and influence but relegated his contribution to 'Art' to a minor level. And what about you? What did you see and feel when you looked at one of Picasso's paintings? Perhaps a jumble of shapes and colours in the same way as a baby is said to see the world as a 'blooming, buzzing confusion'.

Your confusion would be considerable but now imagine what it would be like if you faced this dilemma, if you were totally unprepared, every time you experienced something new. Now we can begin to imagine what a world without attitudes would be like. In this sense, attitudes have been likened to a scientific theory – a frame of reference which saves time by organizing the knowledge available, which has implications for the real world and which changes in the face of new evidence.

In addition to this main function of filtering and ordering our experiences, there are other functions. Attitudes can help us to get what we want. We can attract attention and, more importantly, approval by expressing certain attitudes rather than others. To be accepted by a group one adopts the attitudes of that group whether it involves a lusty appreciation of 'birds and booze' in keeping with the lads in the office or a strong commitment to private enterprise and immigration control in order to fit in with the Monday Club. It must also be remembered that the expression of such attitudes is likely to be praised by fellow group members. In other words, the person will be reinforced for expressing these attitudes and consequently they will increase in frequency – a powerful factor in attitude acquisition, as we shall see later.

Similarly, attitudes can serve to justify or bolster up one's behaviour. For example, a hardened smoker, on encountering the evidence linking cigarette smoking and lung cancer, may well develop an attitude of disbelief about the data. An alternative is to adopt a fatalistic attitude, saying 'Well, you've got to die somehow' or 'If the bullet has got your name on it' or 'A bus might run over me tomorrow'. This is particularly relevant to attitude change for it is commonly found that a change in attitude follows a change in behaviour.

Finally, attitudes can help to relieve personal doubts and inner conflicts which are not attributable to the objects of the attitude. A person having difficulty in finding a job and who is beginning to doubt his ability or his worth may well start blaming it on the government, thereby relieving himself of the responsibility and, hence, the self-doubt.

How do we acquire attitudes?

Now that we know what attitudes are and what functions they serve, we can turn to the question of how we acquire them. One possibility is that we are born with them – that they are innate. In other words, our attitudes are genetically endowed and there is nothing that we can do about them. A new born baby whose father hates pop music and loves gardening is condemned to the same attitudes. The theory in this form not only sounds ridiculous but is manifestly so in the face of the evidence available. Attitudes do not necessarily run in families, although they may do for other reasons discussed later. It is commonplace to find that young student revolutionaries come from solid, conservative, bourgeois backgrounds. The 'generation gap' basically expresses the conflict of attitudes of children and their parents. However, if fear of snakes can be considered as a negative attitude, there is evidence to show that young chimpanzees apparently do display an innate fear of snakes.

A more reasonable version of the theory would be to suggest

that the orientation of attitudes is genetically determined but not the specific attitudes themselves. One general orientation that has been proposed is something as unspecific as 'an aggressive force against persons unlike oneself'. It is suggested that the genes for selfish attitudes will increase in frequency due to survival value. There is, however, no evidence to suggest this and the result of such a process might promise survival for the individual but not necessarily for the species.

There is evidence to suggest that certain aspects of personality are innate. Eysenck and other theorists have put forward the notion that stability as against neuroticism is genetically transmitted. Similarly, a further independent dimension of introversion/extraversion is proposed. Introverts are considered to be more introspective and less socially inclined than the more outgoing, gregarious extravert. If such genetic personality predispositions exist, they might well influence a person's attitudes, but again it is more likely that they will influence the intensity or behavioural outcome of attitudes rather than the direction of the attitudes. Personality may also be influenced by the environment, i.e. aspects of personality may be learned. This learning may well in turn be influenced by the genetic factors. Thus if, for whatever reasons, a person's personality includes a strong tendency towards aggression it will influence his attitudes. An aggressive individual may express his negative attitude towards coloured people by physically attacking them. A similarly aggressive anti-apartheid demonstrator may express his attitudes by physical attacks on white South African sportsmen.

Attitudes can thus be seen to be influenced by genetic factors indirectly but there is little doubt that the origin of specific attitudes lies in experience – attitudes are learned. Some attitudes may be formed on the basis of one experience, other attitudes may take a series of trials to develop. Children often develop fears or negative attitudes to objects very quickly – 'A burned child dreads fire'. A very early experiment by Watson demonstrates the rapid learning of a fear response to a white rat by an eleven-month-old child 'little Albert'. Watson proceeded to produce a loud, banging sound every time little Albert approached the rat. The noise was very frightening to the child and consequently after a few trials his initially positive attitude towards white rats became negative, and he cried every time a rat was produced. This example can be criticized in the sense that some psychologists would argue that this is not an attitude but a specific response. Hard-line behaviourists, however, might argue that specific responses are all that we need concern ourselves with and that the concept of attitude is unnecessary and even meaningless.

Much of the research on attitudes has been concerned with racial prejudice and consequently the development of colour prejudice provides a useful example of how attitudes are learned. There are many influences on the learning of attitudes, some of which have a more direct effect than others. The cultural environment (class, race or religion) often sets the limits on the permitted variation in attitudes, as previously discussed. The main influences on the learning of specific attitudes are the immediate primary groups, the most important of which is the family. Parental attitudes are the major influence on the child's initial attitudes.

Racial prejudice, for example, is not present in very young children but develops as the child becomes more acquainted with his parents' attitudes indirectly and also by their direct teaching. A negative attitude to coloured people may be learned from the parents in various ways. If a child is continually presented with the experience of his parents being angry or tense when discussing the 'blacks next door', he in time will learn this reaction. This process has similarities with a classical conditioning paradigm which would postulate parental anger as the unconditioned stimulus to the child's unconditioned response of fear or some other unpleasant emotional state. The pairing of reference to 'blacks' with parental anger results in 'blacks' becoming a conditioned stimulus to the conditioned response of fear or anxiety.

An operant model also appears to explain the formation of certain attitudes. In hearing the 'blacks' discussed, the child at some point may emit an operant verbal response relating to 'blacks'. If it is a response favourable to 'blacks', parental anger might well act as punishment with the result that favourable responses will be extinguished after several trials. A negative response to 'blacks', however, might well be reinforced just by attracting the parents' attention but is more likely reinforced by their approval ('That's my boy'), both of these, as we have seen, are powerful conditioned social reinforcers.

The most probable way of learning attitudes, however, is by imitation. This consists basically of learning by example, and is considered by many to be an important method by which children learn attitudes. The parents, in expressing negative attitudes about 'blacks', are providing a model for the child's responses. These imitated responses are likely to be reinforced by the parents, which will result in very rapid learning. Thus the child will imitate responses which lead to his getting what he wants, be it approval or more tangible rewards. If the reinforcement is discontinued by, for example, the child moving into a different environment where such attitudes are neither modelled nor reinforced, then new attitudes may well be formed by the child imitating new responses which are reinforced. This often happens when a child leaves home for college.

It is claimed that learning by the reinforcement of free operants is neither an efficient method nor an adequate explanation when one considers the role of imitation. This is brought out clearly in an experiment by Bandura and McDonald (1963) which looked at children's reactions to pairs of stories. Both stories in each pair involved acts resulting in damage, but differed insofar as a selfish act resulted in minimal damage whereas an unselfish act resulted in considerable damage. The children were asked to say which act was the naughtier. (As a point of interest, it has been shown by Piaget that the young child tends to base his decision regarding naughtiness on the degree of damage caused by the act whereas the older child will take into account the intentions of the act.) Their responses to the stories, i.e. their attitudes to the acts, were evaluated and they were then exposed to one of two conditions. Some of the children observed adults expressing attitudes contrary to their own, whereas the other children did not observe adults but were reinforced whenever they expressed attitudes contrary to their initial attitudes. Following this the children were re-tested on the pairs of stories to see what changes, if any, had occurred. The imitation condition resulted in far greater change than the reinforcement condition. This was mainly due to the fact that in the latter condition very few appropriate operants were emitted, i.e. they tended to continue expressing their initial attitudes, and consequently there was little opportunity to shape up the alternative attitudes.

Colour prejudice has been shown to develop as the child

grows older. Harrowitz showed pictures of black and white children to groups of children of different ages asking them to pick out from the pictures children whom they would (a) like to take home (b) like to play ball with (c) like to join their play group. The younger children showed no overall pattern of preference over the three situations but the children in the older groups increasingly with age became more similar in their responses for the three situations. This suggests that as the child grows older he becomes less dependent upon the influence of the situation and builds up a generalization which covers all situations resulting, in this example, in him becoming either positive or negative in his attitude towards coloured children.

A study carried out in a small Tennessee village looked at the ways in which colour prejudice developed. Parents tended to deny that they influenced their children and claimed that they did not need to teach their children not to play with coloured children, implying that this was the natural order of things, that such attitudes were innate. Observation and interviews with children, however, revealed that whereas the very small children played with blacks and whites and were unconscious of racial differences, they were taught by increasingly severe methods not to mix with coloured children. Verbal coercion was apparently insufficient, as a 'whupping' for disobeying the prohibition was very common. 'Cos Mamma says' was the main answer given by the white children when questioned as to why they did not play with coloured children. As they got older, however, they too minimized the influence of their parents on their attitudes and referred to the lustfulness and intellectual inferiority of coloured people. This stereotyping of coloured people is demonstrated in a study in which a class of white children were shown a picture of white people in a library. They were then asked 'What was the coloured man doing?' Their answers indicated that he was doing anything but reading a book – the most common suggestion being that he was sweeping the floor, in keeping with the conventional stereotype.

As the child grows older he will come under the influence of other groups – the peer group being particularly important. A peer group is quite simply a group of peers or persons of similar age and position. A schoolboy's peer group consists of his classmates. The peer group is also important to the formation of attitudes and may change previously acquired attitudes. An

American study showed that Southern students attending Southern schools were far less favourably inclined towards coloured people than Northern students attending Northern schools. A group of Northern students attending a Southern school, however, had attitudes in between the other two groups, suggesting that their attitudes had been influenced by their new community against coloured people.

Thus we can see that a child's attitudes and values are learned in various ways from the family and peer groups. This process whereby a child learns the attitudes and values appropriate to his environment is known as *socialization*. In addition to learning these attitudes, the child also learns another very important set of attitudes – his attitudes towards himself. This is usually referred to as the *self-concept* – the feelings and expectations a person has about himself. These topics will be discussed in detail in later books in this series (C1, C3).

The measurement of attitudes

In our discussion regarding the nature of attitudes we noted that we need to know much more about a person's attitude than its direction. We summed up the various factors relating to differences in the holding of an attitude, by the concept of strength. We can introspect on our own attitudes but how do we go about ascertaining another person's attitudes, how strongly he holds them, how people differ in their attitudes? In order to do any of these we need a means of measurement.

The father of teenage daughters in the 1960s might well have said that he loathed pop groups in general, but within that general 'loathing' his attitudes to specific groups might well have differed. His dislike of the Beatles perhaps paled into insignificance in comparison to his total contempt and disgust for the Rolling Stones. Similarly, the daughters might all have agreed on their intense approval of the Rolling Stones but in reality differed in terms of the strength with which they held the attitude. To assess the differences in attitude both within and between persons requires reliable and valid measurement. A reliable measure will give the same results for the same person in the same situation consistently. Since we want to be sure that our measure is really measuring what we want it to measure, it must also be valid. These are the sort of considerations that must be taken into account in developing a means of measuring attitudes – such measures are commonly called *attitude scales*. A scale provides a means of quantifying attributes or qualities. This will usually involve a choice from a range of numerical values. A very simple scale would involve the teenage daughters being asked to give marks out of ten for various pop groups. Attitude scales commonly consist of a series of statements about which people express their agreement or disagreement along a continuum from 'highly agree' to 'highly disagree'. The statements usually concern a common theme, e.g. attitudes to various methods of child-rearing. The various items will relate to specific aspects of child-rearing and will be scored and added together to give a score indicating the person's general attitude to child-rearing.

The two principal methods involved in scale construction were developed by Thurstone and Likert but since both methods involve complex statistical procedures we will not discuss them here. They will be included in another book in *Essential Psychology* (B3). One of the simplest scales developed involves asking what people would do in certain circumstances. An example of this is the Social Distance Scale (Bogardus, 1925).

The Social Distance Scale was designed to measure a person's attitudes to different races in terms of the 'social distance' which he would want to keep between himself and the given race. The person is asked to state if he would 'willingly admit' members of 'X' race (a) to close kinship by marriage (b) to my club as personal chums (c) to my street as neighbours (d) to employment in my occupation (e) to citizenship in my country (f) as visitors to my country. Bogardus found that over 90 per cent of his American sample would agree to admit Englishmen to all six of these categories. Only 57 per cent would admit Negroes 'to citizenship in my country', dropping to 1 per cent to admit Negroes 'to close kinship by marriage'. Similar responses were found for admitting Jews (54 per cent and 8 per cent respectively).

This is really a sort of quasi-behavioural measure in that it measures what a person believes he would do but not necessarily what he actually does. The commonsense view would be that behaviour is the most valid indicator of attitude. Unfortunately, as we saw in the La Pierre study, behaviour and expressed attitude do not necessarily go together. Behaviour is influenced by many different attitudes and the relative strengths of the cognitive and affective aspects of attitudes which do not necessarily coincide. Sitting in a pub we notice a group of young men laughing appreciatively at every remark a slightly older man makes. From their behaviour we assume that they consider the man to be a great wit. On overhearing the conversation we are not at all impressed by the level of humour and begin to wonder. Suddenly it all becomes clear when we hear a young man say, 'I must remember that one.... By the way, sir, have you completed the new promotion structure yet? ...'

Overt behaviour, therefore, may be an inadequate measure of attitude, but some behaviours are less likely to be affected by conscious control, i.e. physiological changes in the body. It has been shown that there are physiological accompaniments to the experience of emotion – we blush with embarrassment and perspire when we are afraid. Heart rate, perspiration level, muscle tension, etc., can be measured and used as indicators of emotion. This is the basis of the so-called lie detector – a person is asked questions whilst a recording is made of these physiological processes. Lies are thought to be indicated by a sudden change in level which indicates emotional stress. However, such changes could just as easily come about from the fear experienced by the innocent person unjustly accused, as from the lie of the guilty person. The use of such measures in attitude research is open to the same problem. If we observed a sudden leap in the level on our 'lie detector' in response to the question 'Do you approve of homosexuality?', we would not know if it indicated strong approval or strong disapproval. Thus we might get a measure of intensity but not direction, and even the intensity would only be meaningful when compared to the person's responses to other questions. We could not compare individuals in this way as people vary with regard to the base level and rate of change of their physiological processes.

Social attitudes

In a recent public opinion poll West Germans were asked how they would tackle the hippy problem. Should hippies be tolerated, or should they be made to undergo a period of forced labour, presumably in a labour camp of the kind that existed in the Hitler period? Thirty-one per cent of those interviewed were prepared to live and let live but fifty-six per cent favoured the forced labour solution....

In a conversation about work-shy youth the other day, I heard a man who had previously impressed with his tolerance, say: 'Hitler was evil – there's no doubt about that, but you know these labour camps he set up were not a bad idea. There were no long-haired louts about in those days.'

(*Guardian*, 14.9.70, 'Long hair a German badge of courage')

'Fed up ... with the Party Politicians? So you should be! This is what they have done for Britain...., Allowed hundreds of thousands of immigrants into Britain to create unnecessary racial problems and outlawed freedom of speech through the Race Relations Act....

Destroyed our friends while crawling to our enemies.... Tried to make patriotism a dirty word.

Protect the innocent and the law-abiding and stamp out thuggery by ensuring swift and drastic retribution for crime and lawlessness ...

Put Britons first – on housing lists, in jobs and in Education ...

Make Britain a land for decent people – not homosexuals, drug addicts and degenerates – to live in.

If you are 'prejudiced' in favour of your own country – join now. (Extracts from a National Front leaflet)

Fascist Eysenck must not be allowed to speak. In the interests of democracy.... (Extract from a students' union leaflet)

The above extracts are all concerned with expressing social attitudes – attitudes which are concerned with the way society is organized, and which are, therefore, in a sense political. The study of social attitudes has traditionally been concerned with 'prejudice' and 'authoritarianism'. Studies have attempted to determine the nature and extent of prejudiced attitudes and the sort of people holding them. In the 1950s Eysenck (1953) found strong evidence for a generally anti-semitic social attitude. He claims that of his typical middle-class sample 31 per cent believed that 'Jews in their dealings with others are an absolute menace, money-grabbing and unscrupulous', 12 per cent believed that 'Jews corrupt everything with which they come in contact', and 4 per cent believed that 'Jews are the most despicable form of mankind which crawls this earth'. Only 6 per cent

94

believed that Jews had survived persecution because of their many admirable qualities.

Prejudiced people are seen as essentially operating by means of stereotypes and there is a considerable body of evidence to suggest that prejudice in one area is often matched by prejudice in others. Ethnocentrism, the belief that one's own country and social group are superior, results in anti-semitism and negative attitudes towards coloured people. Persons holding such views also tend to believe that war is inherent in human nature, that there should be harsher treatment including flogging for criminals, that conscientious objectors are traitors who should be executed, that sex education is immoral, that religious education should be compulsory, that women are inferior to men, etc. In other words they tend to be patriotic, religious, anti-feminist, sadistic and aggressive.

This phenomenon was investigated by Adorno *et al.* (1950), who devised the 'F Scale' to assess these sorts of attitude which tend to come together in what they called the *Authoritarian Personality*. The 'F Scale' required persons to indicate degrees of agreement or disagreement with statements of the following kind:

Obedience and respect for authority are the most important virtues children should learn.

People can be divided into two distinct classes: the weak and the strong.

From their research findings they argued that there is a syndrome of authoritarian attitudes which can be identified as making up the largest part of some people's personalities. The characteristics of the 'Authoritarian Personality' are hypothesized as the following:

He has a great concern for authority relationships showing extreme deference to his superiors whilst dominating those below him. Adorno et al refer to this as the 'bicyclist's personality' – 'Above they bow, below they kick'.

He adheres strictly to the rules of society, shows great respect for conventional behaviour, values and morality and displays aggression towards those who flout these values. 'It is now evident that anyone not in complete agreement with the views of this newspaper is a fascist' (quote from the leader of an American newspaper).

He is anti-introspective and tough-minded and is preoccupied with the division between the weak and the strong. He is ego-centric and displays rigidity of thought processes.

He denies his own 'immoral' feelings but suspects immoral be-haviour in others, usually of a sexual nature. He is convinced of the rightness of his morality and is obsessed with the decadence around him.

He is cynical about the human race and exploits others whilst complaining of being personally exploited. He has both sadistic and masochistic tendencies.

He is intensely prejudiced and intolerant towards minority groups.

The syndrome basically describes what we commonly call fascism, although this term is now so debased that it tends to refer to anyone who is not quite as liberal as you are. Even so it is interesting to note that in 1938 a Nazi psychologist, Jaensch, published his ideas regarding the character of the ideal man, or J-type, contrasted with the S-type. The J-type – the tough minded, anti-introspective Hitlerian ideal – corresponds very closely to the Authoritarian Personality. There is also a distress-ing similarity between certain aspects of the Authoritarian Per-sonality syndrome and the policies of extreme right-wing groups in this country, as may be seen from the extracts from the National Front leaflet quoted earlier.

Rokeach (1960), in his work on *dogmatism*, extends the con-cept of authoritarianism further. Dogmatism is defined as 'closed-mindedness'. Someone who is extremely dogmatic works from a set of highly organized attitudes which have usually been derived from authority in some form or another and which are extremely resistant to change in the face of new information. This leads him to avoid close relationships with those whose attitudes are dissimilar to his own as they threaten his belief system. Rokeach's forty-item attitude scale correlates with the F scale significantly. Unlike the authoritarian, however, the dog-matic person is not necessarily right wing in his politics. The dogmatic individual can be right or left wing and is charac-terized by the extremeness of his views rather than their politi-cal direction.

Eysenck (1954, 1957), arguing from the results of his Social Attitude Inventory, proposes a model that incorporates the possibility of authoritarianism of the left or the right. He claims that there are two factors underlying social attitudes; radicalism/conservatism and tough/tender mindedness. Tough-minded people are realistic, worldly and aggressive compared with tender-minded people who are idealistic, moral and submissive. These two opposing orientations are strongly associated with extraversion and introversion respectively. The Social Attitude Inventory measures both factors, including items such as:

Ultimately private property should be abolished and complete Socialism introduced.
The death penalty is barbaric and should be abolished.
We should believe without question all that we are taught by the church.

Eysenck claims that the major political groups do indeed read from left to right in terms of increasing conservatism but that the communist and fascist groups are both characterized by extreme tough-minded authoritarianism. This explanation makes more sense of the apparent similarity of the regimes imposed by Hitler and Stalin; and also why student left-wingers can be both extremely radical and extremely authoritarian, as witnessed by their determination that 'fascist Eysenck [ironically enough] must not be allowed to speak'.

Recently a new scale has been devised by Wilson and Patterson (1968) to measure conservatism. The Conservatism Scale attempts to measure the same sorts of social attitude previously collectively referred to as dogmatism, authoritarianism, fascism, etc., and hence it is claimed that the high scorer on the test, the extreme conservative, will display the following characteristics:

1 religious dogmatism
2 right-wing political orientation
3 insistence on strict rules and punishment
4 ethnocentrism and intolerance of minority groups
5 preference for conventional art, clothing and institutions
6 anti-hedonism – a tendency to regard pleasure as bad
7 superstition and resistance to scientific progress.

The test aims to avoid ambiguity and confusion engendered by having to evaluate long attitude statements by the use of labels or catch-phrases. Instead of responding to 'The death penalty is barbaric and should be abolished', the individual merely indicates whether he favours or believes in the 'death penalty'.

The test consists of fifty items including 'school uniforms', 'striptease shows', 'patriotism', 'modern art', 'working mothers', 'suicide', 'white superiority', 'fluoridation', 'female judges', etc. Typical scores on the test (maximum score 100) include university students 32·57, professional 43·76, unskilled workers 47·24, typists 53·75, businessmen 58·40 and housewives 60·98. The test has confirmed previous findings that women tend to be slightly more conservative than men and that conservatism increases dramatically with increasing age.

Changing attitudes

Attitudes may change or be changed in a variety of ways depending upon the information and experiences a person acquires. Attitudes may change involuntarily as a result of a new experience or may have been deliberately changed by a skilled propagandist. In this section we will look at the various ways in which attitude change is brought about.

As we have already said, the membership of groups influences the attitudes which a person will acquire, especially the family and the peer group. Hence, changes in group membership may result in attitude change. In an American study carried out at a very liberal girls' college, it was found that the attitudes of the girls became progressively more liberal as they became increasingly assimilated into the social 'scene' of the college; girls who were not assimilated showed much less change towards liberalism. Situational changes can also affect attitudes – in times of economic crisis prejudice towards 'out-groups' increases. In times of unemployment there is a strong increase in negative attitudes towards immigrants.

Attitude change may also be brought about by changes in behaviour. On occasions, changes in behaviour are forced on individuals by authority in some form or another. Due to a housing shortage American whites were forced to live in an integrated public housing project. This change in behaviour rapidly resulted in more favourable attitudes being expressed towards Negroes. Similarly, contact with the object can cause attitude change. In terms of prejudice, experience with the object results in a realization that the stereotype is incorrect. There may also be changes in the object itself which will lead to a change in attitude towards it. A young man's strong positive attitude towards his attractive, sophisticated fiancée may change rapidly if after marriage she slouches around the house in curlers, house-coat and slippers.

Various models have been proposed to account for and predict attitude change. They have all been based on a common assumption – that a person's system of attitudes is a balanced system and consequently a change in any one component leads to imbalance. Attitude change is a means of re-establishing the balance and harmony of attitudes. The various theories and models have referred to principles of balance, congruity, symmetry, consistency and consonance. We will look at only the last of these theories as an example of the general approach – the other theories will be detailed in another text in this unit, B3.

The theory of *cognitive dissonance* (Festinger, 1957, 1962) is probably the theory which has had the greatest impact on social psychology and has led to considerable research. Its influence is now waning, however. Festinger postulates that there is a drive towards consonance of attitudes and attitude components. Any occurrence which breaks down this consonance leads to a state of cognitive dissonance which is experienced as a form of tension which is uncomfortable. This tension motivates the person to redress the balance by changing an attitude or attitude component so that it is in line with the rest of the system. In passing we might note that Benn and others have formulated simpler and, arguably, more objective behavioural models accounting for this phenomenon but which will not be discussed here.

This theory centers around the idea that if a person knows various things that are not psychologically consistent with one another, he will, in a variety of ways, try to make them more consistent. Two items that psychologically do not fit together are said to be in a dissonant relation to each other. The items of information may be about behavior, feelings, opinions, things in the environment and so on. The word 'cognitive' simply emphasises that the theory deals with relations among items of information.

Such items can of course be changed. A person can change his opinion; he can change his behaviour, thereby changing the information he has about it; he can even distort his perception and his information about the world around him. Changes in items of information that produce or restore consistency are referred to as dissonance-reducing changes.

Cognitive dissonance is a motivating state of affairs. Just as hunger impels a person to eat, so does dissonance impel a person to change his opinions or his behaviour. . . . (Festinger, 1962)

We have previously referred to the hardened cigarette smoker who encounters the evidence linking smoking and cancer. In this situation the person is likely to experience dissonance, i.e. a conflict between his behaviour, smoking, and the knowledge that it can cause death by lung cancer. In order to reduce this dissonance the person has two options – he can change the behaviour or the knowledge. If he cannot bring himself to stop smoking he is likely to choose the latter alternative, and change the nature of the knowledge by expressing disbelief at the facts or expressing a fatalistic lack of concern for death. Festinger (1957) cites a survey which shows that 29 per cent of non-smokers, 20 per cent of light smokers, but only 7 per cent of heavy smokers believed that a link between smoking and cancer had been established.

On another occasion Festinger had the opportunity to try out his theory in a real-life setting. A quasi-religious group had formed in 'Lake City', led by a medium supposedly in touch with extra-terrestrial beings from the planet Clarion. The medium, Mrs Keech, subsequently received a communication to the effect that Lake City, along with the rest of the continent, would be destroyed by a great flood on a certain date. However, Mrs Keech's group, the 'Seekers', were to be saved from the disaster by the 'Guardians', who would rescue them by means of flying saucers. Festinger and his co-workers infiltrated the group in order to see how the group members would react to the dissonance created by the imbalance between reality and their beliefs.

As the date of the 'disaster' fell during the vacation, many student followers had returned to their homes but a number of followers had remained in Lake City to face the disaster together at Mrs Keech's house. Many of the followers had indicated their commitment to their belief in the end of the world by giving up their jobs, possessions, etc. Moreover, the movement was characterized by its lack of interest in publicity or in making converts.

On the set day, the Lake City group awaited the arrival of the flying saucer due at midnight.

The clock chimed twelve, each stroke painfully clear in the expectant hush. The believers sat motionless. . . . Midnight had passed and nothing had happened . . . there was no talking, no sound. People sat stock still, their faces seemingly frozen and expressionless. (Festinger *et al.*, 1956)

The group eventually gave way to despair and Mrs Keech broke down into tears. Not long afterwards, however, another 'message' was received – the cataclysm had been called off due to the faith of the 'Seekers'.

Needless to say, this 'explanation' was avidly received by the group. They immediately began to publicize their explanation and began to solicit converts to their beliefs. The 'Seekers' who had spent the night on their own, however, in isolation from the group, either gave up their beliefs or greatly reduced their respect for Mrs Keech.

Festinger's own prophecy regarding the subsequent behaviour of the 'Seekers' was fulfilled. As he had predicted, their commitment was so great that rejection of their beliefs on the basis of the evidence would result in more dissonance than they could deal with. Also Festinger took account of the group factor – a group which consisted of people in the same position. If they could each convince each other of their continued belief and also seek out and convert others, then the dissonance could be reduced by the social support in spite of the evidence to the contrary.

It is perhaps important to stress that dissonance is engenedered when one element is psychologically contrary to the other. As a sixth former I was very impressed by the novels of Kingsley Amis. Imagine my dismay, however, when I discovered a letter by him to a magazine expressing somewhat reactionary attitudes to American involvement in Vietnam. I experienced dissonance not because the elements of Amis as a splendid novelist and Amis as a reactionary are logically opposed but because I experienced them psychologically as being opposed. Having all the correct, left-wing liberal attitudes myself I could not see how a reactionary (who was, therefore, unintelligent) could write such superb novels. I do not remember ever resolving the dissonance satisfactorily except that with increasing age, perhaps my own conservatism increased allowing me to read Kingsley Amis with an easy conscience!

5
Groups, conformity and helping

In response to questioning about Darwin's theory of evolution, the man in the street will confidently refer to 'survival of the fittest' as being the major force involved. It is extremely unlikely that he will refer to what Darwin considered equally important, the value of cooperation. It is not so much a case of 'weakest to the wall' but more likely a case of 'united we stand, divided we fall'. Darwin, in *The Descent of Man* (1871), expressed this in the following way:

As man is a social animal, it is almost certain that he would inherit a tendency to be faithful to his comrades, and obedient to the leader of his tribe; for these qualities are common to most social animals. He would from an inherited tendency be willing to defend, in concert with others, his fellow men; and be ready to aid them in any way which did not too greatly interfere with his own welfare, or his own strong desires.

Darwin's commitment to the inherited nature of cooperation would not be supported by many psychologists today. Cooperation does have survival value, however, and as such would be likely to continue to be transmitted in some form from generation to generation.

Man's evolution, like that of many other species, has placed a strong emphasis on the value of the group, so it is no surprise that much of what concerns social psychology is man as a member of groups. Hunting bands, warrior tribes, armies, committees, families, bridge clubs, sewing circles, social classes, political parties – all of these groups involve the phenomenon of

102

man inter-acting with others. Social psychologists have been interested in determining the major factors influencing group behaviour, asking how a group is different from the sum of its constituents, finding out the rules operating in groups. This area of study has come to be known as 'Group Dynamics', referring to the forces acting on, within and emanating from the group.

Group dynamics

The study of groups has been approached in many ways. In this section we will review some of the principal areas of research with groups. A major concern has been with establishing the relative efficiency and the satisfaction of group members with the structure of groups formed for the purpose of communication.

Leavitt (1951) imposed different *communication networks* on five-person groups meeting around a table. The groups were asked to solve problems under different conditions of group organization. The different groups were structured to vary the channels of communication open to members. (The four structures investigated are shown in the figure below.) In the circle net each member can communicate only with those group members in his immediate left and right whereas in the wheel net the person at the hub (C) can communicate with all four of the other members but they can only communicate with him. The chain is similar to the circle except that the persons on each end of the chain (A and E) can only communicate with one other person and not each other; similarly, the Y resembles the wheel except that the person at the 'hub' (C) cannot communicate directly with the person at the base of the Y (E).

Each person has one piece of information and in order to solve the problem set, it is necessary to know what information every member has. The person (C) at the hub in the wheel and the Y obviously has more access to information, having more channels available, than any other member and so tends to function as the leader in collating the available information. The study revealed that the wheel and Y-type groups solved the problems much more quickly than the chain or circle groups. Over a series of trials they rapidly developed an efficient system based on the coordinating leader. Consequently the person at the hub (C) enjoyed his job much more than the peripheral members. Similarly, circle-group members also enjoyed their job more than the peripheral members of the wheel- and Y-type groups. The conclusion is, therefore, that groups based on a leader, i.e. centralized networks, are much more efficient in terms of problem solving but at the risk of reduced job satis-

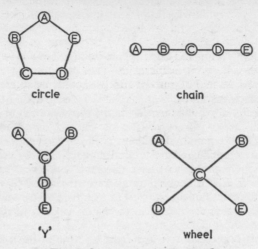

Fig. 2 *Communication networks*

faction by peripheral group members. Subsequent research has shown, however, that more difficult problems are solved more efficiently by circle-type groups. In everyday life, decisions are often dependent upon information being collected via hierarchical structures similar to the Y and wheel or by committees which are an example of another sort of network, the 'comcon', wherein everybody, theoretically, has direct access to everyone else.

As we have seen in these studies, the persons at the hub had 'greatness thrust upon them'; they were forced to become leaders by virtue of the structure imposed. Even persons who would certainly not have assumed leadership status in other circumstances were accepted as leaders by the other group members. As Gibb (1969) has said, 'Leadership is a function of personality. It is also a function of the social system. But more basically it is a function of these two in interaction.'

104

Leaders are said to be more dominant, more masculine (whatever that might mean) and more intelligent than rank-and-file group members. The leader's intelligence, however, especially in children, must not be too superior to that of other members. When there is a great difference in I.Q. between potential leader and led, either the relationship does not form or soon disintegrates. Leaders also are apparently more salient, they stand out from the crowd, and are less neurotic and better adjusted compared with their subordinates. They prefer to keep themselves at a distance and tend not to mingle socially with the people they supervise. Surprisingly, they have also been found to be more deviant. They are less likely to abide by conventional norms and conform less.

Perhaps we might note in passing the consideration of leaders as models. Leaders, occupying the role they do, have power and prestige; they are powerful dispensers of reinforcers. Leading a group involves changing the behaviour of the group members separately and collectively – in other words the leader needs to induce learning. This may be considered as being carried out by his modelling of the desired behaviour which is imitated by group members who both respect him and are dependent on him.

Leadership is one of the attributes of groups which may be investigated by the use of sociometric techniques. *Sociometry* is a technique devised by Moreno (1953) to study and measure the structure of groups in terms of the nature of the relationships between group members. By means of sociometric techniques one can produce *sociograms* which show the patterns of 'feeling' that exist amongst the individuals comprising a group. The basic technique involves simply asking each member of the group with whom they would most like to associate for a specific purpose; similarly, the group may be asked to make negative choices. Various strategies have since been advocated, including asking each member to rank the other members in order of preference, but we will concern ourselves only with the basic technique.

The method allows one to see at a glance those members who are highly regarded by the others, the 'stars', and those who are ignored or rejected, the 'isolates'. One can also see reciprocal dyads or triangles who form 'mutual admiration societies' or cliques. It is to be stressed that although sociograms may be constructed from simple 'who do you like and dislike?' approaches, the structure of sociograms may well vary if one varies the criterion of assessment. It is preferable to specify as accurately as possible the dimension on which the group members are to be evaluated in order to obtain clear judgements. If one asks 'Who do you like best?' the subject could reasonably say he likes all the group members for different reasons. Similarly, the group members must have known each other for a reasonable length of time in order to have formed impressions of each other. A further very important point is that group members must be reassured that their confidences will be respected and that their choices will not be revealed.

Purely as an example of this technique we may look at a demonstration sociometric study I carried out several years ago on a group of psychology students who had been meeting regularly for weekly seminars. As it was 'just for fun', the criteria selected were not terribly serious, nor was it rigorously carried out. The group consisted of four males and four females. They were asked to record two positive and two negative choices for each of the following criteria:

(a) The person who would have the greatest impact on psychology
(b) The person with whom you would most like to work on a psychology project
(c) The person whom you would most like to invite to a party.

From their replies three sociograms were constructed of which the following figure is one, showing only the positive choices for criterion (a):

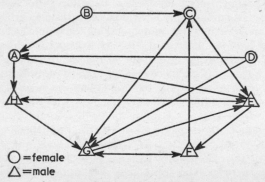

○ = female
△ = male

Fig. 3 *A typical sociogram*

106

The negative choices followed a similar reverse pattern. The sociogram shows that the two males E and G were considered to be the psychological stars and the two females B and D very much the isolates. G and F apparently share a mutual admiration as do H and E. The sociogram for criterion (c) showed a very different social structure. The previously isolated Miss B became a star when it came to parties and perhaps not so curiously, the previous psychological star Mr G became a party isolate. It would appear that the group had, in a sense, two leaders, a social leader Miss B and an intellectual leader Mr G. This ties in with Bales's work on leadership in groups which suggests that two leaders are common, the 'task oriented' or 'ideas specialist' and the 'best liked man'. However, Bales (1955) found that these two types of leader complemented each other and functioned as a team but in this study reciprocal negative arrows were found between Miss B and Mr G on each of the three sociograms for the three criteria! The mid criterion (b) of working on a psychology project resulted in a mixed bag of both positive and negative choices for both Mr G and Miss B. Obviously for a work partner one needs someone who is both able and with whom one can get on. To fit this criterion, Miss C unexpectedly rose to become a star.

Yet another aspect of leadership is the effect of different styles of leadership on the behaviour of groups. Kurt Lewin carried out what is now regarded as a classic study on 'group climate' (Lewin, Lippitt and White, 1939). Lewin and his co-workers trained boys' club leaders to play three different types of leadership role, termed 'autocratic', 'democratic' and 'laissez-faire'. The autocratic leader gave orders, discouraged communication between the boys and was non-objective in his criticism and praise of the boys' work. The laissez-faire leader opted out of the group as much as possible, he did not give orders or make suggestions unless specifically asked. The democratic leader embodied the all-American ideal – he helped the boys plan, made suggestions, listened to their suggestions, was concerned for their welfare and participated in the life of the group. The leaders were very well trained so that their individual performances were very similar. The leaders moved from one club to another every six weeks, changing their leadership style with each move. The clubs all consisted of groups of ten-year-old boys of similar intelligence, socio-economic status, etc. The behaviour patterns within the groups under different leaders were carefully recorded and conclusions drawn about the sort of behaviour found under the three different styles of leadership.

More work was achieved under 'autocratic' conditions than under 'democratic' conditions and least under 'laissez-faire'. However, group solidarity, originality, motivation to work, approval of the leader, enjoyment and cooperation were all higher in the 'democratic' condition. Morale was very low in the 'autocratic' condition, and more aggressiveness and destructiveness was found. Under the 'laissez-faire' condition not only was little work done but the general atmosphere was of apathetic chaos. Most of the boys preferred the 'democratic' leader and all of those who dropped out did so under 'autocratic' conditions. One or two of the boys did, however, prefer the autocratic regime, in particular one boy whose father was an army officer. Perhaps we should bear in mind, however, that this study was carried out in the United States where democracy is at least preached if not always practised, and hence we might expect both experimenter and subject effects.

An area of investigation which is still popular in social psychology is group decision-making. One's experience of committees leads one to suspect that decisions made by groups are usually rather unadventurous and safe but experiments on this topic have repeatedly shown that groups tend to take *riskier* decisions than would be made, on average, by the individual members comprising those groups. This phenomenon is usually referred to as a 'shift to risk' or *'risky shift'*.

The early work on this is admirably reported by Brown (1965). Stoner, a graduate student working under Wallach and Kogan, used a set of problems devised by his supervisors for the purpose of measuring how much risk individuals were prepared to take. He proceeded to ask groups first to determine how much risk they would each personally take and then to form a consensus group decision on the degree of risk to be advocated. The problems consisted of twelve situations one might encounter in everyday life. In each situation the central character is faced with a decision as to whether to take a more or less risky course of action. The subject's task is to evaluate the situation and to indicate the lowest probability of success upon which he would be prepared to gamble before advocating the riskier but more attractive option. An example of a typical problem is the following:

Mr A, an electrical engineer, who is married and has one child, has been working for a large electronics corporation since graduating from college five years ago. He is assured of a lifetime job with a modest, though adequate salary, and liberal pension benefits upon retirement. On the other hand it is very unlikely that his salary will improve much before he retires. While attending a convention, Mr A is offered a job with a small, newly founded company which has a highly uncertain future. The new job would pay more to start and would offer the possibility of a share in the ownership if the company survived the competition of the larger firms.

Imagine that you are advising Mr A. Listed below are several probabilities or odds of the new company proving financially sound. Please check the lowest probability that you could consider acceptable to make it worthwhile for Mr A to take the new job. (Kogan and Wallach, 1964)

The subject has to select whether he would demand a 1, 3, 5, 7, 9 or 10 out of 10 probability that the company will prove sound, before advocating that Mr A should take the new job. An extremely cautious person would demand 10/10, i.e. total certainty that the company will succeed, whereas a very risky individual would advise that Mr A take the plunge if the company only has a 1 in 10 chance of succeeding.

It has been found repeatedly, regardless of sex of subjects or size of group, that the group decision after discussion is consistently more risky than the mean or average of the members' individual decisions. Moreover, when the individuals were asked to record their individual judgements, again after the group decision-making, it was found that many subjects moved to a more risky decision.

The critical question is 'What causes risky shift?' and many alternative explanations have been proposed. One possibility is the diffusion of responsibility hypothesis. This suggests that, because of the possibility of bad consequences, an individual will be reluctant to take the sole responsibility for making a risky decision in case it results in failure. In a group, however, the responsibility is no longer his alone, but will be spread over all the group members, and hence a greater risk may be taken. Another theory argues that high risk-takers are more persuasive in argument than low risk-takers and hence swing the rest of the group members over to their side. Certainly high risk-takers are identified as being more persuasive by other group members in subsequent interviews but this may merely be a supposition based on the fact that the decision went their way. Yet another explanation is that our society values risk within reason and hence everyone wants to feel he is as risky as the next man. When a low risk-taker enters into group discussion he finds he is below average in terms of risk-taking and so increases his risk to the average level. This results in a higher group mean to riskiness. But equally, it may be argued, if we only value risk 'within the average level. This results in a higher group mean for riskiness to the average level also? There is also the conformity theory, a topic which will be discussed in the next section. If there is a tendency to conform to the group mean or the norm, again we are faced with the problem of why high risk-takers do not conform as well as low risk-takers. A possible explanation is that cautious, low-risk-taking behaviour is indicative of general conservatism which has been shown to be linked to a greater tendency to conform.

Groups are also becoming increasingly popular as a means for 'personal growth'. Group therapy as a psychotherapeutic technique has been practised for many years, and works on the assumption that people with 'problems' who get together can learn from each other how to face up to those problems. The techniques and types of group vary considerably, some having definite leaders, others being leaderless. 'Sensitivity training' groups, however, are for apparently normal people who desire to become more 'personally aware'. Smith (1971) defines the function of such groups in the following way:

The essence of sensitivity training is this: that our effectiveness as individuals is intimately bound up with our relations with others; that through life we learn certain ways of relating to one another, but that this process may be speeded up by assembling groups of people who talk freely and openly concerning all aspects of their relationships with the others; and that the relationships which evolve in this intense, and in one sense artificial, setting have relevance to a person's everyday experience subsequently.

The radical nature of this essentially educational approach is twofold. First, it assigns responsibility for learning to the individual trainee. The group leader's task is not to teach, but to

110

set up conditions where trainees can learn if they choose to.... Second, the approach stresses the importance of a person's feelings as something especially worth understanding (as exemplified in learning how to express anger – or control it – or learning how to recognize anger in others) ....

The two main types of sensitivity training groups are the human-relations training group, or T-group, and the more recent encounter group. Aronson (1972) differentiates the two approaches:

... the term T-group refers to the more conservative, more traditional group, in which the primary emphasis is on verbal behaviour and the group discussions are almost exclusively confined to the here and now.... The term 'encounter group' is most often associated with the more radical wing of the human-potential movement; the activities of such groups often include a heavy dose of such non-verbal procedures as touching, body movement, dance, massage and so on.

It is very difficult to determine what the specific aims of such groups are and why their advocates consider them to be a preferable way of achieving those aims. Talking to people who attend such sessions can be rather irritating; their statements of aims tend to be rather vague and if you press them further the reply is that you must experience it for yourself. In my limited experience of such groups, this involved us all making minor criticisms of each other, quickly stressing afterwards that even so we thought each other to be really nice persons. There is a more serious side to this, however. I understand that, over time, the honesty builds up with an increasing emphasis on the expression of emotion. This often leads to emotional outbursts such as fits of anger or floods of tears. As we argued in the chapter on social learning, this cathartic approach is based on the assumption that it is beneficial to release pent up emotions. The fact that such emotional outbursts increase over sessions plus the emphasis on the benefits of catharsis suggest that what is in fact happening is the teaching of 'emotional behaviour'. The behaviour is modelled and imitations of it are reinforced so that such behaviour is likely to increase in frequency. It could be fairly argued that such behaviour is not likely to lead to the solving of personal problems and that it might be more advantageous to model and reinforce more positive coping behaviours to deal with emotional problems. In passing we might

111

note that unconditional sympathy to a person in distress may act as a very powerful reinforcer of emotional behaviour causing it to increase, thus decreasing the possibilities of more adaptive behaviour being learned. For sympathy to be effective in helping solve emotional problems, it should be conditional upon positive attempts at coping behaviour by the distressed person. It is possible that such groups in reinforcing the emotional behaviour itself might be functionally acting contrary to their aims.

We now turn to an examination of the effect of groups on human behaviour in terms of conformity and willingness to help others, especially persons in distress; we will also consider a related topic – obedience to authority.

Conformity

In our discussion of the 'risky shift' phenomenon I mentioned, rather glibly, the possibility of an explanation in terms of 'conformity'. The term conformity, however, is a rag-bag term covering several similar, related but distinct, phenomena which are all concerned with the effect of the influence of other people on a person's behaviour.

Less closely related phenomena include *audience* and *co-action effects* (reviewed in Zajonc, 1966). Apparently ability to perform a simple task is improved by the presence of an audience whereas the performance of more complex tasks is adversely affected. Co-action refers to the situation where many people are performing the same task at the same time as each other but not cooperatively. This has the effect of increasing output. Similarly, tolerance for electric shock is greater under these conditions.

The term conformity refers to the situation whereby a person is influenced to perform a certain act by seeing another person or, more likely, persons performing that behaviour. As we shall see, however, the reasons for conformity behaviour of this type ocurring may be very different so that we may identify several, discrete phenomena within the global term conformity. Firstly, however, we will consider *conformity proper*, a field of research most closely associated with the name of Solomon Asch, who emphasizes the immediate social relevance of conformity:

In society we become dependent upon others for understanding, feeling and the extension of the sense of reality. But this relation places a particular demand upon the participants of social action. If our dependence and trust are to have solid ground ... each must contribute out of his understanding and feeling. Often this condition is not fulfilled. The story of the emperor's new clothes is one example of the baseless consensus produced by the failure of each to make his proper contribution ... we are appalled by the spectacle of the pitiful women of the middle ages who, accused of being witches by authorities they never questioned, confessed in bewilderment to unthought-of crimes. But in lesser measure we have each faced denials of our feelings and needs ... a theory of social influences must take into account the pressures upon persons to act contrary to their beliefs and values ... we need to go beyond the mild and painless aspects of group influence. (Asch, 1952)

One of the earliest experiments on conformity was conducted by Sherif, who made use of the visual illusion known as the autokinetic effect; the phenomenon whereby a static point of light viewed in a dark room appears to move after a while. Sherif asked his subjects to estimate the distance and direction of the light's movement which, as it is merely an illusion, is totally subjective and hence greatly varying reports are normally received. However, when his subjects were instructed to discuss their estimates, this rapidly led to a consensus of opinion. The group appeared to exert a pressure to conform so that when the subjects were returned to the darkened room they all agreed on the direction and distance covered by the light.

Asch's basic experimental procedure involved the subject being asked to make judgements in a group which consisted, unknown to him, of the experimenter's confederates. The group are informed that they are to judge the length of a target line against three lines of differing lengths, one of which is the same length as the target line. The other two lines varied by appreciable amounts. The confederates, all of whom give their judgements first, are instructed to give the same incorrect answer on certain trials. The subject is faced with the dilemma, on such trials, of making public his disagreement with the other group members or of agreeing with their answer which he knows to be false. In control conditions, without other group members being present, subjects achieved over 90 per cent accuracy in matching the lines but in the conformity condition subjects went along with the majority on over a third of the trials in which the group deliberately selected an incorrect alternative.

This effect was shown even more dramatically when the difference between the lines was increased to seven inches so that control subjects were almost 100 per cent accurate in their judgements. There was almost the same amount of conforming observed, and without, it must be stressed, any coercion being employed. The confederates announced their judgements publicly and firmly but neither argued nor looked surprised when the subject disagreed with them.

In de-briefing sessions following the experiments, Asch told the subjects the real purpose of the study and asked for their comments on how they felt when they were faced with a majority who contradicted the evidence of their senses. All the subjects were aware of the disagreement between themselves and everybody else in the group. An initial reaction, commonly found, was the belief that the disagreement could only be temporary. Later on in the trials they began to formulate hypotheses to account for the continual discrepancy. Doubts as to whether they had understood the instructions were common. Were they perhaps comparing width, not height, or was it an optical illusion? Several concluded that their eyesight must be failing. They were also concerned about the unpredictability of the group from trial to trial so that they became confused. One subject commented, 'I was sure they were wrong but not sure I was right.' The subjects admitted to considerable self-doubt and discomfort and the pressure of an increasing compulsion to give the incorrect majority decision the closer it came to their turn. Subjects often felt sure they were right but went along with the majority anyway, occasionally voicing doubts or small protests. Some subjects told the experimenter that they yielded so as 'not to spoil your results'.

Various modifications were then made to the experimental procedure so as to determine some of the factors affecting conformity. Size of the group was an obvious variable to investigate. Experiments showed that when the group consisted of only one confederate and one genuine subject, the subject remained independent and did not conform. When a further confederate was introduced, conformity began to appear about 14 per cent of the time, and when a third confederate was added conformity rose to over 30 per cent. Further increases in group size, however, had little effect in increasing conformity. Conformity could be greatly reduced, however, by introducing a partner for the subject who consistently gave the correct answer. The presence of only one other person agreeing with the subject is apparently enough to strengthen his resistance to conformity. If the partner begins to join the majority, however, and make incorrect judgements in line with the rest of the group, conformity by the subject increases again. The effect of having a partner does reduce conformity if the partner leaves the group, as the subject, now facing the majority alone, is now much less likely to conform. Conformity may also be reduced by contriving for the subject to arrive 'late' and, so as not to interrupt the ongoing procedure, asking him to record his decision in writing. As the subject no longer has to make public his disagreement with the majority, conformity is considerably reduced.

Crutchfield (1955) extended Asch's work and devised a new procedure whereby conformity could be investigated more efficiently. Five subjects are installed in adjoining booths so that they cannot see each other but can all see slides projected onto a screen in front of the group. Inside each booth are switches by means of which each subject can communicate his decisions and also an array of lights which each subject is led to believe indicates the judgements of the four other subjects. In actuality the lights are controlled by the experimenter who can, at will, give the impression that the other group members are in complete agreement with each of the subjects at the same time. Each subject is led to believe that he is the last to respond on each trial. Thus it can be seen that subjectively the experience is similar to that encountered by Asch's subjects.

Crutchfield found very similar results to Asch but was able to use a far wider range of materials. The most important of these was the judgement of attitude statements such as 'I believe we are made better by the trials and hardships of life'. In control conditions virtually no disagreement with this statement was found but when the lights were rigged so as to give the impression that the other four group members disagreed, over 30 per cent of the subjects expressed disagreement. Even more disturbing is the item, 'Free speech being a privilege rather than a right, it is proper for a society to suspend free speech whenever it feels threatened'. In control conditions only 15 per cent of subjects agreed, but in the conformity situation 58 per cent endorsed this attitude.

Crutchfield also investigated the sort of variables which influence conformity and in particular what sort of person is likely to resist conforming. Non-conformers are said to display more intellectual effectiveness, ego strength, leadership ability, and maturity of social relationships. They lack feelings of inferiority, authoritarian tendencies and rigidity of thought. The non-conformer is efficient, expressive, aesthetic, active, natural, unpretentious, self-reliant and is not submissive, narrow, inhibited or lacking in insight. Females apparently conform more than males but this may be a reflection of the fact that women are also more conservative than men; conservatism/authoritarianism being a strong determinant of conformity. Adult women who had attended college were, however, less conforming than their male counterparts. Surprisingly, there is little difference between occupations in terms of the amount of conformity displayed by persons in different occupations. Fifty American military officers displayed conformity 37 per cent of the time but equal conformity was found in samples of engineers, writers, scientists and architects.

Asch, pointing to the social implications of research of this kind, concludes:

Life in society requires consensus as an indispensable condition. But consensus, to be productive, requires that each individual contribute independently out of his experience and insight. When consensus comes under the dominance of conformity, the social process is polluted and the individual at the same time surrenders the powers on which his functioning as a feeling and thinking being depends. That we have found the tendency to conformity in our society so strong that reasonably intelligent and well-meaning young people are willing to call white black is a matter of concern. It raises questions about our ways of education and about the values that guide our conduct.

Yet anyone inclined to draw too pessimistic conclusions from this report would do well to remind himself that the capacities for independence are not to be under-estimated. He may also draw some consolation from a further observation: those who participated in this challenging experiment agreed nearly without exception that independence was preferable to conformity.

(Asch, 1955)

Zajonc (1966), reviewing this research on conformity, presents the other side of the coin and considers conformity in terms of vicarious learning by imitation.

On the other hand, conformity, like imitation, has some important adaptive benefits. Scare one bird, and the whole flock will fly away. Each member of the flock need not be threatened individually. The survival value of such a process cannot be overlooked. Responding to the behaviour of others may be less discriminating and less independent, but waiting for the appropriate cue could be disastrous. When you see flood victims fleeing the impending disaster, you need not wait for the flood to come to your doorstep before running away.

Imitation is a significant device in learning. The opportunity to imitate saves the imitator the trouble of selecting from the totality of the environmental stimulation the cues relevant to his behavior at the moment. Others accomplish this task for him. Imitation prompts us to make appropriate responses that otherwise might not be made. This is extremely important, for if one is to acquire a response tendency, the response must be repeatedly reinforced. In order for reinforcement to occur, the response must first be made. If a given response has a low probability of occurrence, it will have a low probability of being reinforced, and hence a low probability of being learned.

The theoretical link between imitation and conformity is examined by Wheeler (1966), who isolates several phenomena which might all loosely be termed conformity. He reserves the term conformity strictly for the Asch effect and seeks to differentiate it from *behavioural contagion*, his principal concern. An example of this latter phenomenon might be a man in a non-smoking compartment on a train who desperately wants to smoke. On seeing another traveller light a cigarette, the man disobeys the sanction and also lights a cigarette. A similar situation exists when one reaches for a cigarette during a conversation. It is likely that other smokers will also begin to smoke. In this situation there is no sanction against smoking and it is an example of *social facilitation*. Bandura would refer to this as the eliciting effect of a model. Wheeler argues that 'Imitation may be considered a generic term subsuming contagion, conformity and social pressures, and social facilitation.'

The three separate phenomena may be clearly distinguished even though the actual behaviour may be the same in each case, i.e. that the model's behaviour is imitated. Social facilitation

117

may be said to occur when a person initially feels neither restraints not instigation towards performing a certain behaviour.
Following the behaviour of the model, the possibility of performing the behaviour is made apparent, causing the subject to
overcome possible inertia and perform the modelled behaviour.
In the case of conformity, the subject initially wants to behave
in a certain way (i.e. give the correct judgement) but following
the behaviour of the model(s) (giving an incorrect judgement)
the subject now experiences a conflict between which of the two
behaviours to adopt. He may now feel restrained from behaving
in the way he wants to and copy the model's behaviour. Behavioural contagion differs from this in that the subject wants to
perform a certain behaviour but initially feels restrained from
doing so. The model performing that behaviour has the effect of
lessening the restraint and hence the subject now feels free to
behave as he wanted to. As Wheeler points out, behavioural
contagion may, on occasions, be directly opposed to conformity
and may prove to be the more powerful of the two phenomena.
As an example he points to the Asch experiment where the
subject wants to give the correct judgement but feels restraints
against doing so because the majority are unanimous in their
(incorrect) judgement. He therefore tends to give the incorrect
judgement, but when a partner is brought in the situation
changes. The partner performs the behaviour the subject wants
to perform, thereby reducing the restraints, and contagion occurs, with the result that the subject stops conforming.

Other examples of behavioural contagion, reported by
Wheeler, include disobeying traffic signals and the dangers of
double-dating. Lefkowitz, Blake and Mouton carried out an experiment on the conditions under which pedestrians will disobey
a traffic signal instructing them to wait before crossing the road.
Pedestrians violated the prohibition more often in the presence
of a model who ignored the prohibition than when the model
was absent or obeyed the signal. Perceived status of the model
also had a significant effect. If the model was dressed to re-
present a person of high status (i.e. wearing a suit, white shirt,
polished shoes etc.) more subjects imitated his behaviour than
when the same model was dressed in a denim shirt, dirty trou-
sers and scuffed shoes. This ties in well with the point made
earlier in Chapter 2, that models are more likely to be imitated
if they apparently have the power to reinforce, which a high-

status person is more likely to have. Similarly, Bandura and Walters have argued that adolescents are more likely to engage in sexual intercourse during double-dating. Given that an adolescent girl wants to have sex with her boyfriend but feels moral restraints against doing so, these restraints will be reduced if she sees her girl-friend engaging in this behaviour and contagion may result. However, as Wheeler makes clear, the girl-friend must be an appropriate model. If she is notoriously promiscuous, her behaviour is much less likely to be imitated. The apparent sexual morality of the model should ideally be slightly higher than that of the observer.

Obedience to authority

Under his hand there was a dial with a lever on top and figures running round the face. . . . Without any movement except a slight movement of O'Brien's hand, a wave of pain flooded his body. . . . O'Brien drew back the lever on the dial. The wave of pain receded almost as quickly as it had come.

'That was forty,' said O'Brien. 'You can see the numbers on this dial run up to a hundred. Will you please remember, throughout our conversation, that I have it in my power to inflict pain on you at any moment and to whatever degree I choose? . . .'

(*1984*, George Orwell)

The cat and mouse game over, Big Brother decides that Winston needs 'help'. This is the equivalent of 'Ludoviko's technique', by means of which Winston will be normalized to the mores of Ingsoc in *1984*. But how could O'Brien do such a thing? Is he insane? Brainwashed/conditioned? Just plain evil? Maybe one or all of these things, but equally maybe none. Maybe he's just like you and me and the ordinary, everyday men and women who helped to exterminate millions of Jews in the death camps of Nazi Germany. The above quote from *1984* is remarkable not only for its manifest purpose, to conjure up the horrors of totalitarianism, but also because it basically describes the procedure adopted in a series of experiments on obedience by Stanley Milgram (1974) at Yale University. This series of experiments has been called 'the most morally significant research in modern psychology'.

Milgram's basic research question is 'If x tells y to hurt z, under what conditions will y carry out the command of x and under what conditions will he refuse?' To investigate this he initially brought volunteer subjects in pairs into his laboratory at Yale University and paid them $4.50 each prior to their taking part in the experiment. He informed them that they were to be subjects in a study investigating the effect of punishment on the learning of word pairs; one subject was to act as the teacher and the other as the learner. Although a coin was tossed to decide who was to be the learner, this was always rigged so that the learner was always a confederate of the experimenter who had been trained to act in a very convincing way. It was explained to the teacher that it was his job to teach the learner a list of word pairs. The teacher was to give the first word and the learner had to attempt to respond with the other correct word of the pair. Should he fail, the teacher (the naive subject) was instructed to administer an electric shock to him. The learner was a fifty-year-old man who in passing remarked that he had a heart condition.

The teacher was then shown the experimental set-up including the shock generator, a highly authentic looking piece of machinery with thirty switches on it incrementing in 15-volt units from 15 volts to 450 volts. He was given a sample shock as a demonstration and instructed that he was to start at 15 volts and administer a shock for the first mistake and to increase the severity of the shock by 15 volts each time the subject subsequently failed to give the correct answer. The learner is then strapped into the 'electric chair' in the next room and an electrode is attached to his wrist.

Milgram was concerned to find out at what point the teachers (the real subjects) would stop giving the shocks. Forty psychiatrists whom he asked to predict the results of his experiment argued that most subjects would refuse to continue fairly early on and that virtually no one would administer the highest shock (450 volts). During the course of the learning programme, the learner (who is of course not in reality wired up to the shock generator) convincingly increases his distress as the severity of the shocks increases. By making many mistakes, the required voltage rapidly reaches 75 volts, whereupon the learner moans and grunts. By 150 volts he is asking to be excused from the experiment and, as the voltage continues to rise, screams and says he cannot stand the pain and can no longer respond. At the point labelled 'Extreme Shock' on the generator, the learner stops responding and bangs on the wall, begging to be released. As the shocks rise to 450 volts, 'Danger! Severe Shock' level, no response, not even shouting or banging, is heard. During the course of this procedure, if the teacher shows reluctance or refuses to continue, the experimenter merely says 'Please continue'. Subsequent refusals are met with 'The experiment requires that you continue', 'It is absolutely essential that you go on' and as a last resort the chilling, 'You have no choice but to go on'.

The subjects consisted of men aged between twenty and fifty drawn from all walks of life, who lived in New Haven, Connecticut. There was no evidence to suggest that they were not a sample of normal human beings but a staggering 62 per cent of these subjects obeyed the experimenter right up to the 450 volts, 'Danger – Severe Shock' level! This study has been repeated many times under many different conditions. For example, it may be argued that seeing as the subjects knew that the experiment had the backing of the prestigious Yale University, they would think it unlikely for it to be allowed if anyone was going to be seriously hurt whilst taking part. However, the results were very similar when Milgram replicated the study in a seedy set of offices in Bridgeport, totally unconnected with Yale University.

The behaviour of many of the subjects as they continued to increase the severity of the shocks became increasingly bizarre. They began to show signs of emotional strain, including sweating, trembling, lip-biting, groaning and stuttering. Even more disturbing were the subjects who broke out into hysterical laughter. An observer who watched one subject gave the following report:

I observed a mature and initially poised businessman enter the laboratory, smiling and confident. Within 20 minutes he was reduced to a twitching, stuttering wreck, who was rapidly approaching a point of nervous collapse. He constantly pulled on his ear lobe, and twisted his hands. At one point, he pushed his fist into his forehead and muttered: 'Oh, God, let's stop it.' And yet he continued to respond to every word of the experimenter and obeyed to the end. (Milgram, 1963)

Another man constantly repeated, 'It's got to go on. It's got to go on', and many attempted to reduce the dissonance engendered by their behaviour with such remarks as 'He was so stupid and stubborn he deserved to get shocked'. One subject described his feelings in a post-experimental interview in the following way:

I had about eight more levels to pull and he [the learner] was really hysterical in there and he was going to get the police, and what not. So I called the professor three times. And the third time he said, 'Just continue,' so I give him the next jolt. And then I don't hear no more answer from him, not a whimper or anything. I said, 'Good God, he's dead; well, here we go, we'll finish him.' And I just continued all the way through to 450 volts....
... I faithfully believed the man was dead until we opened the door. When I saw him, I said, 'Great, this is great.' But it didn't bother me even to find that he was dead.... I believe I conducted myself ... obediently, and carried on instructions as I always do.... I did my job.

Milgram modified his experimental procedure in various ways to investigate the factors determining obedience. When the learner was actually in the same room as the teacher and his anguish was clearly visible as well as audible, 40 per cent of subjects still obeyed to the end. 30 per cent of subjects were even prepared actually to force the learner's hand down onto a metal plate in order to give him the shock. As the presence of the experimenter was decreased in proximity, however, obedience was reduced. When the experimenter was out of the room and gave his orders by telephone, obedience dropped to 22 per cent and many subjects cheated by administering lower voltage shocks than was required. This is, however, but small consolation in view of the previous evidence of a large-scale willingness to inflict severe pain on other human beings.

Other experiments incorporated more members of the 'teaching' team who were also confederates of the experimenter. When 'fellow teachers' refused to continue administering the shocks, only 10 per cent of the subjects obeyed to the end. This may be viewed in terms of behavioural contagion. The subject wanted to refuse to continue but felt restrained by the experimenter's authority; a model refusing to continue, however, reduced this restraint and allowed the subject to do what he wanted. However, when the subject was a member of a team and did not have to administer the shock but merely administer the word-pair test, over 95 per cent of the subjects obeyed to the end. They excused their behaviour by claiming that it was the responsibility of the person who actually administered the shock. As Milgram (1974) says,

It is psychologically easy to ignore responsibility when one is only an intermediate link in a chain of evil action but is far from the final consequences of the action. Even Eichmann was sickened when he toured the concentration camps, but to participate in mass murder he had only to sit at a desk and shuffle papers. At the same time, the man in the camp who actually dropped Cyclon-B into the gas chambers was able to justify his behavior on the grounds that he was only following orders from above. Thus there is a fragmentation of the total human act; no one man decides to carry out the evil act and is confronted with its consequences. The person who assumes full responsibility for the act has evaporated. Perhaps this is the most common characteristic of socially organised evil in modern society.

As previously mentioned, this research has been criticized on ethical grounds in view of the suffering caused to the subjects who believed that they were responsible for severe shocks to a fifty-year-old man with a heart condition. Each subject was, however, very carefully de-briefed after the experiment and was reassured by the learner that he had not suffered any pain at all. Apparently over 80 per cent of subjects stated that they were glad that they had taken part in the experiment and many felt that they had gained something from the experience. Only 2 per cent regretted taking part in the experiment.

Critics of Milgram have pointed out, however, that he has in a sense also fallen victim to the dangers of obedience. In submitting to the 'authority of science', it is argued, he himself was prepared to inflict psychological pain on others. It is my opinion, however, that it is unethical to carry out bad research. It is difficult to see how this research could have been carried out without inflicting pain as it is extremely unlikely that role-playing by the subjects would have produced similar results. It is vital that we are made aware of the facts regarding social phenomena if we are to attempt to change society for the better and on these grounds such experimental procedures may be justified. Milgram's conviction regarding the value of his research and its immediate social relevance characterizes his writing:

> The results, as seen and felt in the laboratory, are to this author disturbing. They raise the possibility that human nature, or – more specifically – the kind of character produced in American democratic society, cannot be counted on to insulate its citizens from brutality and inhumane treatment at the direction of malevolent authority. A substantial proportion of people do what they are told to do, irrespective of the content of the act and without limitations of conscience, so long as they perceive that the command comes from a legitimate authority. If in this study an anonymous experimenter could successfully command adults to subdue a fifty-year-old man, and force on him painful electric shocks against his protests, one can only wonder what government with its vastly greater authority and prestige, can command of its subjects. (Milgram, 1965)

Helping others

In 1964, Kitty Genovese was brutally stabbed to death in a residential area of New York City at 3 a.m. The incident lasted half an hour, during which time Kitty screamed and cried for help and the murderer, after initially running away, returned to stab her again. Thirty-eight people witnessed the attack from the safety of their apartments and not one attempted to intervene, go to her aid or even call the police. Subsequent interviews revealed that the witnesses had not felt apathetic, they were genuinely horrified, but still they had not helped.

Several years ago, a girl friend and I, walking down a busy street in Derby after an evening at the cinema, noticed a man slumped, apparently unconscious, in a shop doorway. As the crowds hurried by, almost treading on him, we stopped in some confusion. Perhaps he'd had a heart attack; perhaps he was dead. Neither of us knew what to do and looked appealingly at passers-by. No one stopped but eventually a man assured us in passing, 'It's alright, it's O'Flaherty; he's drunk again.' We knew the name, it appeared frequently in the *Telegraph* on charges of being drunk and disorderly, and with one last look we too joined the passers-by. But the man continued to haunt us; he might still have been ill and even if he was drunk he could hardly remain there all night. Our finer feelings were not matched by our behaviour, however. Perhaps, we thought, he might have become violent when he came round; and if he had been really ill surely someone else would have stopped and helped. This, of course, is the crucial factor; the fact that no one else was helping reduced our desire to help, even though we had initially stopped.

The Kitty Genovese atrocity aroused considerable public comment and media speculation. One can imagine a tense face on the T.V. screen demanding, 'Is this just the tip of the iceberg of the increasing alienation of modern man in contemporary society?' Ignoring this sort of journalistic sociologism, Bibb Latané and John Darley proposed a much more down to earth explanation; that no one attempted to help simply because there were so many other people who were also watching the attack. This may be viewed in at least two ways. First of all we could interpret it in terms of diffusion of responsibility, one of the explanations we put forward to account for risky decision-making by groups. If only one person is on hand when help is required, it is his sole responsibility to help but this decreases as the number of potential helpers increases. Secondly, there is the conformity explanation, the fact that the group, i.e. for each individual the other persons present, was setting the appropriate behaviour, *not* helping. A person who helps in this situation is going against the group and may also possibly make a fool of himself if the victim refuses his help or jumps up and says 'April Fool' or whatever. Given that we are all seeking the reinforcement of social approval or at least trying to avoid social disapproval, in going against the group we are not likely to be reinforced and may be punished if we make fools of ourselves. An interesting point about the second view, the conformity theory, is the consideration of what would happen if one person stopped to help. Arguing from behavioural contagion theory, and assuming that people really want to help, we would predict that on seeing someone else help, others would be more likely to offer help also. This was not borne out in my experience with the drunk, apart from the passer-by who bothered to tell me who the man was, but then this was hardly a conclusive experiment. Latané and Darley (1970) have, however, conducted several studies on helping behaviour which clarify the issue by experimentally investigating the hypothesis that the probability of someone helping a victim decreases if there are several potential helpers on the scene.

In a very ingenious study they persuaded college students to discuss the problems of living and learning in the urban environment with other students. Each subject was led to believe that he would be conversing with other students over an intercom system, as in order to preserve complete anonymity they would all be placed in separate rooms. Each student was to take his turn and say exactly what he felt, secure in the knowledge that only the other students could hear him and they would never see him. There was, however, only one real subject involved per discussion; the other 'students', who varied in number (either one, two or five), were in fact only tape recordings of the experimenter's confederates. After each 'student' had spoken once, including the subject, the first confederate, who had previously mentioned he was prone to seizures, began to speak again during the course of which he apparently actually experienced a seizure and called out for help. The independent variable was the size of discussion group the subject thought he was in (two persons only, three persons or six persons) and the dependent variables were attempting to help by opening the room door and the time delay between hearing the attack and opening the door.

If the subject thought he was the only other person in contact with the 'victim' he was far more likely to help. 85 per cent of subjects in this condition opened their doors compared with only 31 per cent in the six-person condition; the three-person condition fell between the other two. These results were confirmed by the respective mean times taken to open the door, i.e. subjects in the two-person condition responded fastest. This ties in exactly with Latané and Darley's hypothesis that the more people there are present in an emergency the less likely it is that any one person will help. Neither sex, personality nor background influences helping behaviour in experiments of this kind, but modifications to the procedure have revealed two important influences. Prior acquaintance with the 'victim', experimentally induced by the subject 'accidentally' meeting the victim just prior to taking part in the experiment, had the effect of increasing the probability of the subject helping. Similarly, if two people who already know each other are both acting as naive subjects in the same group, there is also a greater likelihood of help being offered. Both of these variables appear to derive their effect from a common factor, that their failure to help will be observed by someone who knows them which might lead to later criticism. As another experiment described later will show, people tend to help if they think they will not get away with not helping. In the above two cases, either the 'victim' who now knows the subject or the subject's friend is a potential critic who may not let the subject get away with his non-helping behaviour without adverse comment later on.

In a more naturalistic experiment (but which was not a field study), Latané and Rodin (1969) investigated reactions to a lady in distress. College students were asked by a female investigator to fill in a questionnaire either alone or in pairs. A short while after leaving the room, the experimenter simulated an accident. Through the open door the subjects heard (by means of a tape recording) the sound of the experimenter climbing on to a chair, followed by a scream, a crash and then moaning to the effect that she could not move her foot as her ankle was damaged. Once again, the hypothesis was substantiated; 70 per cent of those 'witnessing' the accident alone volunteered help as against only 20 per cent of the subjects in pairs. Faced with these sorts of findings, it is no longer a surprise that no one offered to help Kitty Genovese. She still serves as a chilling reminder, however, of what to expect if one suddenly meets with an accident in view of many observers.

Darley and Batson (1973) investigated what they felt would be other relevant variables. Previous studies had shown that expected predictor variables such as authoritarianism, social responsibility etc. were but poor predictors of helping behaviour, so they decided to look at religious orientation, effect of previously discussing helping and degree of 'hurry'.

Forty students at Princeton Theological Seminary acted as subjects in the experiment, half of whom read a passage on future job prospects while the other half read the parable of the Good Samaritan. Subjects were then told to report to another building to record a short talk on the subject of the passage they had read. Each subject was told: (a) that he was late for this appointment already ('high hurry' condition) or (b) that the person could record his talk as soon as he arrived ('intermediate hurry') or (c) that he had plenty of time to get over to the other building ('low hurry'). Whilst crossing to the other building, each subject encountered a supposed 'victim' slumped in a doorway, who was moaning or coughing and who apparently needed help. Sixteen of the forty students stopped to offer some sort of assistance. Only the 'hurry' variable was a statistically significant predictor of helping behaviour in this situation. 63 per cent helped in the low hurry condition, compared with 45 per cent in the intermediate condition and only 10 per cent in the high hurry condition. Religious orientation apparently affected quality rather than quantity of helping, i.e. it affected the sort of help offered. However, it is curious that on average only 40 per cent of these committed Christian students stopped to offer help to a person in need. Even a prior reading of a biblical example of helping did not increase their helping in real life. 'Indeed, on several occasions, a seminary student going to give his talk on the parable of the Good Samaritan literally stepped over the victim as he hurried on his way.' It seems extremely callous that the only factor determining whether they stopped or not was whether they could afford the time – apparently 'ethics becomes a luxury as the speed of our daily lives increases'. Darley and Batson argue, however, that the need for help did not register with some students due to the time pressure, whereas others chose not to stop in the 'hurry' conditions 'because the experimenter, whom the subject was *helping*, was depending on him to get to a particular place quickly ... conflict rather than callousness can explain their failure to stop.' This argument, however, closely resembles ethical criticisms of Milgram's work. These subjects are also putting obedience to science first. In the same way as Milgram, in the cause of science, was prepared to upset people by leading them to believe they had inflicted severe pain on another human being, these students were prepared to ignore a person manifestly needing their help in order to help instead the experimenter, by being on time for his experiment.

Piliavin *et al.* (1969) carried out a field study into helping by New Yorkers (remembering Kitty Genovese) on the city's underground rail system. The 'victim' collapsed in a carriage containing several people and remained outstretched on the floor. The results showed that people were extremely eager to help. Someone offered immediate help in over 95 per cent of the trials when the person was manifestly ill, and even when he was apparently drunk he was offered help by someone on 50 per cent of the trials. In this study, helping did not appear to be influenced by number of people present as there was no difference in helping behaviour between crowded and virtually empty trains.

The main explanation offered for this failure to replicate previous findings is that unlike passers-by, the underground travellers could not 'pass by on the other side', i.e. they could not escape from the 'victim'. They either had to help or be seen to be not helping; they could not just avoid the situation. In the same way as subjects who had prior acquaintance of the victim or who were known by a co-subject in Latané and Darley's studies, people in this set of circumstances could not get away with non-helping behaviour. If we cannot rely, then, on 'fellow feeling' to initiate help in emergencies, we might possibly be able to shame people into helping by refusing to let them get away with not helping. Perhaps the thing to do in an emergency requiring more than one person's help is to pick someone out of the passers-by and demand their help, thus making it impossible for the person to be able to ignore the need for help.

Moving on from a victim in distress to theft, Latané and Elman (in Latané and Darley, 1970) investigated the conditions under which people would report a theft. In a laboratory study subjects witnessed a theft whilst waiting for an interview. In one condition the subject saw the only other person present, a confederate of the experimenter, steal some money from a desk; in the other condition two subjects saw the confederate carry out the crime. From a commonsense point of view one would predict that the subjects in the latter condition would be more likely to intervene or report the theft as it would be two against one and thus they would be more likely to be believed or, if the need arose, be more able to overpower the thief.

The subjects saw the thief blatantly steal from an envelope on the receptionist's desk while she was out of the room. The receptionist had made sure that they knew that the envelope contained a considerable amount of money. The subjects had the opportunity to confront the thief or to report him when he had left for his 'interview'. Before the actual subjects were interviewed, it was also made obvious that the theft had occurred by the receptionist suddenly 'missing' the money and asking if the subjects knew anything about it.

In spite of the obviousness of the theft, 52 per cent of subjects in the 'alone' condition claimed not to have noticed it, compared with 25 per cent of the 'paired' subjects. The experimenters who observed the reactions of all subjects were convinced that most of the subjects did actually see the theft, though many, on seeing the beginning of the theft, appeared to avoid seeing its completion. As for actual spontaneous reporting of the crime, 24 per cent in the 'alone' condition reported it as against only 19 per cent in the 'paired' condition. Looking only at those who admitted noticing the theft, 50 per cent of 'alone' noticers reported it compared with only 25 per cent of 'paired' noticers.

The most important findings of this study are that (a) few people were willing to report the crime whether alone or with others and (b) many people refused to admit or believe that they had actually seen the crime take place. In spite of the blatant theft, excuses included 'It looked like he was only making change' and 'I thought he took the money by accident'. The experimenters concluded that the crime was likely to be reported slightly but not significantly less often when two persons witnessed it.

In a similar filed study carried out in 'real life', customers alone or in pairs observed one or two husky young men steal a crate of beer from an off-licence when the manager was absent from the counter. The number of 'robbers' had little effect on reporting but a higher percentage of witnesses reported the theft in this study than in the lab study, 65 per cent of witnesses on their own reported it as against only 56 per cent of witnesses in pairs. Both studies confirm, however, that more than one witness to a crime does not increase the probability of its being reported. Moreover, it appears that many people are reluctant to 'grass' even on manifest criminals. In the second study only 20 per cent of all subjects volunteered the fact that the beer had been stolen without any prompting from the shop manager.

To end on a bright note, however, in our discussion of the paucity of helping behaviour in modern everyday life, let us look at a study showing when people are more likely to help. Isen and Levin (1972) report that feeling good leads to helping even when the good feeling is totally unrelated to the helping. In a field study, people entering a public telephone booth either did or did not find a ten cent piece in the coin return slot. On leaving the box they encountered a female confederate of the experimenter who 'accidentally' dropped a manilla folder full of papers. The dependent variable was whether the subject helped pick up the papers or not. The results were absolutely clear out. 87·5 per cent of those who had received the ten cent piece helped pick up the papers against only 4 per cent who had not received the ten cent piece. Another experiment in which students in a library were or were not given cookies prior to being asked to take part in a psychology experiment, showed that those who had been given cookies were more likely to volunteer and for a longer period.

These results offer at least some relief from the gloom engendered by the generally found unhelpfulness of people, but the practical value may be limited. What does it mean in real terms? One is reluctant to face the fact that help is only likely to be forthcoming if the potential helper is in a good mood. Kitty Genovese was in no position to make people feel good while she was being stabbed to death. Perhaps a 'gentleman of the road' whom a friend of mine met in London had the right idea. His technique was to approach students with 'I can see you're an intellectual and I read a good bit myself. Now do you think you could see your way to helping a fellow student with the price of a cup of tea?'

Social psychology and society

In this last chapter of the book we have discussed conformity, obedience and helping behaviour at some length. I make no apology for the added emphasis given to these topics, as they are all particularly socially relevant areas of research demonstrating social influences on social behaviour. The results in general hardly serve to increase our faith in human nature but they do help us to form more realistic judgements of what we can expect in social situations. A greater understanding of social phenomena such as these may also enable us to attempt to change society, or the forms of social behaviour within it, for the better.

It is interesting to note that whilst most liberal-minded people would agree that what is needed is less mindless conforming, less unquestioning obedience and more positive helping, these were all offered as part of the package deal presented by the 'hippy ideal' which was spawned in the Indian summer of 1967. Most people rejected it and of those who initially accepted it, many later turned, in disillusionment, to more direct forms of action, epitomized by the battle of Grosvenor Square. If a knowledge of the facts is more powerful than a belief in ideals, however, it may still be possible to change the

131

direction of society by more peaceful and more scientific means.

As I write this (1974) the media, in their summer 'silly season' when parliament is in recess, are currently 'concerned' with two main topics, both concerning the social behaviour of young people, football violence and the Windsor Pop Festival. The reaction of the authorities and the public to both topics is basically the same, i.e. 'stamp it out'. Stamp out the violent behaviour of these so-called football fans; stamp out the pop festival organized by these drug-crazed hippies. The search for possible cures of football violence currently occupies considerable speculation. Apart from the old chestnut of national conscription, there have been proposals for fencing the fans in, keeping rival fans apart, issuing identity cards and forcing convicted offenders to carry out social work on Saturday afternoons. Why, ask the press, the public and the authorities, do they indulge in this senseless violence? Why can't they take their pleasures in something more constructive? Possible appealing alternatives might include music, dancing, camping, meeting new people. And where can they do all of these things? You've guessed it, at a pop festival. Not only that, but pop festivals have become renowned for their relative lack of violence and the goodwill and harmony engendered. Why, then, were the police called in to 'stamp out' the festival at Windsor and why do the general public and the authorities tend to be against all such festivals? The answer to this is a complex one. Firstly, many of the festivals are held illegally, as was Windsor. Permission was not granted by the Windsor Great Park authorities. This particular festival was, however, allowed to continue for six days before it was broken up. The second point is 'drugs', a word that strikes terror into the hearts of the public. Without wishing to minimize the harmfulness of hard drugs, it must be said that society's attitude to marijuana is curiously illogical. Scientific investigations have shown that the effects of its use are neither extreme nor harmful but it is still illegal and possession, especially with the intention of selling it, can lead to severe fines, if not imprisonment. Alcohol, with all its known adverse effects on health and behaviour, is, however, freely available even to young people below eighteen; pubs are rarely 'busted' for illegal drinkers. Here again is an example of the illogicality of the attitude of the authorities responsible for social control, in the face of the evidence.

The point I am basically trying to make is that social problems are being investigated by a science of social psychology. Society, however, or at least those in authority, seem loath to act on the evidence available. In the light of knowledge that is available, some social problems are being dealt with illogically. Society does not want young people to indulge in violent behaviour at football matches but discourages young people from indulging in peaceful behaviour at pop festivals. Who would you prefer to meet on a dark night – a crowd of drunken football fans or a crowd of doped 'hippies' returning from a pop festival?

A social psychological analysis of the situation would take into account the forces maintaining or influencing the social behaviour in question. It would then argue that if you wish to change one form of behaviour and/or maintain another then you must structure the contingencies accordingly. As we have already said, footballers appear to serve as powerful models to their impressionable fans. If less violent behaviour occurred on the pitch, less might well occur off it among the fans. Soccer heroes, moreover, could be used as positive models. Not only could they model less violence on the field they could also model disapproval of violence off the field, on television and when meeting the fans. Manchester United are to be applauded for initiating this sort of practice with their fans who have possibly the worst reputation in football. Similarly, committed, non-violent supporting by fans could be reinforced by means of a yearly competition for the supporters' club with the best record.

The police are another group who need to be made more aware of the effect of their modelling on the behaviour of young people. Their behaviour has often been described as 'brutal' at demonstrations and pop festivals. The *Daily Mirror*, whilst not agreeing with the illegal Windsor festival, did note that 'several police were restrained by senior officers as they bundled fans away. There were a couple of baton charges and young parents with small children found themselves in the front of the battle. ... One man said, "People have been fighting back because the police are using exceptional force when they drag people away. They're not content just to arrest people. They have to beat them up as well." ' Another spokesman made the point that 'They [the police] have over-reacted and have caused enough ill-feeling against police to last these young people a lifetime'.

The same article referred to the behaviour of the hippies themselves. Apparently the sort of behaviour they were modelling and reinforcing is summed up in a hippy's comment, 'We love each other. We feed each other. We help each other.'

Given that the festival was illegal, however, and had several bad points (e.g. virtually non-existent sanitation arrangements), could not similar legal festivals be organized jointly by the authorities in collaboration with young people who have experience of running them? If we want to avoid mob violence, why not reinforce peaceful crowd behaviour? Appropriate models of, for example, helping behaviour appear to be available already among hippies; why do the police not model more appropriate behaviour? Moreover, the police could reinforce appropriate behaviour whilst helping to prevent undesirable behaviour. A more tolerant attitude towards marijuana, for example, would certainly facilitate control of dangerous hard drugs, as witnessed by the fact that at Windsor hippies claimed, 'We had *our* policemen to keep the hard drug pushers out'. They are often forced into identifying with the people who do use and sell them, however, by the attitude of the police who appear not to differentiate.

This one example of a social 'problem', the social behaviour of young people, has been discussed at some length in order to demonstrate my argument that social psychology is not only relevant but can also be directly applicable to the understanding and solving of social problems. Having established what sort of social behaviour is prevalent in society and how behaviour may be learned and modified by imitation and reinforcement, we now have to decide what sort of social behaviour we want. By controlling the models and contingencies of social reinforcement, I believe that it is possible to change social behaviour for the better; I believe it is possible to shape a better society through the science of social psychology.

Suggested further reading

In general

Aronson, E. (1972) *The Social Animal*. San Francisco: W. H. Freeman. A very readable account of socially relevant areas of research within social psychology.

Brown, R. W. (1965) *Social Psychology*. New York: Free Press. Probably still the best, if now slightly dated, textbook on social psychology available.

Lindren, H. C. (1969) *An Introduction to Social Psychology*. New York: John Wiley. A very thorough coverage of social psychology including a consideration of social learning.

Chapter 1: *Introduction*

Miller, S. (1975) 'Experimental Design and Statistics', *Essential Psychology*, A7. London: Methuen.

Swingle, P. (1973) *Social Psychology in Everyday Life*. Harmondsworth: Penguin

Chapter 2: *Social Learning*

Bandura, A. (1967) The role of modelling processes in personality development. In *The Young Child: Reviews of Research*. National Association for the Education of Young Children. Reprinted in Foley, T. M., Lockhart, R. A. and Merrick, D. M. (eds.) (1970) *Contemporary Readings in Psychology*. New York: Harper and Row.

Skinner, B. F. (1948) *Walden Two*. New York: Macmillan.

Skinner, B. F. (1953) *Science and Human Behaviour*. New York: Macmillan.

Walker, S. (1975) 'Learning and Reinforcement', *Essential Psychology*, A3. London: Methuen.

Chapter 3: *Language and Communication*

Argyle, M. (1972) *The Psychology of Interpersonal Behaviour*. Second edition. Harmondsworth: Penguin.

Gahagan, J. (1975) 'Interpersonal and Group Behaviour', *Essential Psychology*, B2. London: Methuen.

Green, J. (1975) 'Thinking and Language', *Essential Psychology*, A6. London: Methuen.

Parry, J. (1969) *The Psychology of Human Communication*. London: University of London Press.

Robinson, W. P. (1972) *Language and Social Behaviour*. Harmondsworth: Penguin.

Chapter 4: *Attitudes and Prejudice*

Festinger, L. (1962) 'Cognitive dissonance', *Scientific American*. Reprint no. 472 (October edition).

Reich, B. (1975) 'Values, Attitudes and Behaviour Change', *Essential Psychology*, B3. London: Methuen.

Rokeach, M. (1972) 'The nature of attitudes?' In Sills, D. L. (ed.) *Encyclopaedia of the Social Sciences*. New York: Collier-Macmillan.

Warren, N. and Jahoda, M. (1973) *Attitudes* (2nd edn.). Harmondsworth: Penguin.

Chapter 5: *Groups, Conformity and Helping Behaviour*

Asch, S. E. (1955) 'Opinions and social pressure', *Scientific American*. Reprint no. 450 (November edition).

Gahagan, J. (1975) 'Interpersonal and Group Behaviour', *Essential Psychology*, B2. London: Methuen.

Glenn, F. (1975) 'The Social Psychology of Organizations and Institutions', *Essential Psychology*, B4. London: Methuen.

Latane, B. and Darley, J. M. (1973) *The Unresponsive Bystander: Why Doesn't He Help?* New York: Appleton-Century-Crofts.

Milgram, S. (1974) *Obedience to Authority*. London: Tavistock Publications.

Stacey, B. (1975) 'Psychology and the Social Structure', *Essential Psychology*, B5. London: Methuen.

References
and Name Index

The numbers in italics following each entry refer to page numbers within this book.

Adorno, T. W., Frenkel-Brunswick, E., Levinson, D. J. and Sanford, R. N. (1950) *The Authoritarian Personality*. New York: Harper and Row. *95–6*

Allport, F. H. (1954) Attitudes in the history of social psychology. In G. Lindzey (ed.) *Handbook of Social Psychology*, Vol. 1. Reading, Mass: Addison Wesley. *77*

Argyle, M. (1972) *The Psychology of Interpersonal Behaviour*. (2nd edn.) Harmondsworth: Penguin. *66–9, 71*

Aronson, E. (1972) *The Social Animal*. San Francisco: W. H. Freeman. *111*

Asch, S. E. (1952) *Social Psychology*. New York: Prentice Hall. *113*

Asch, S. E. (1955) Opinions and social pressure. *Scientific American*. Reprint no. 450 (November edition). *112–15, 116*

Bales, R. (1955) How people interact in conferences. *Scientific American*. Reprint no. 451 (March edition). *107*

Bandura, A. (1962) Social learning through imitation. In Jones, M. R. (ed.) *Nebraska Symposium on Motivation*. Lincoln: University of Nebraska Press. *47, 117, 119*

Bandura, A. (1967) The role of modelling processes in personality development. In Foley, T. M., Lockhart, R. A. and Merrick, D. M. (eds), *Contemporary Readings in Psychology*. New York: Harper and Row. *46–8*

Bandura, A. and McDonald, F. J. (1963) Influence of social

reinforcement and the behaviour of models in shaping children's moral judgements. *Journal of Abnormal and Social Psychology* 47 : 274–81. *89*

Bernstein, B. (1961) Social structure, language and learning. *Educational Research 3* : 163–76. *57–9*

Bernstein, B. (1971) *Class, Codes and Control*, Vol. 1. London: Routledge & Kegan Paul. *56–60*

Bloom, L. (1970) *Language Development: Form and Function in Emerging Grammars*. Cambridge, Mass : M. I. T. Press. *59*

Bogardus, E. S. (1925) Measuring social distances. *Journal of Applied Sociology 9* : 299–308. *92*

Brown, R. W. (1965) *Social Psychology*. New York : Free Press. *13, 14, 61–2, 63, 108*

Brozek, J. (1966) Contemporary Soviet psychology. In O'Connor, N. (ed) *Present Day Russian Psychology*. Oxford : Pergamon Press. *31*

Calvin, A. D. (1962) Social reinforcement. *Journal of Social Psychology 66* : 15–19. *45*

Crutchfield, R. S. (1955) Conformity and character. *American Psychologist 10:* 191–8. *115–16*

Darley, J. M. and Batson, C. D. (1973) From Jerusalem to Jericho : a study of situational and dispositional variables in helping behaviour. *Journal of Personality and Social Psychology* 27 : 100–8. *127–8*

Darwin, C. (1871) *The Descent of Man*. New York : Appleton. *15–16, 102*

English, H. B. and English, A. C. (1958) *A Comprehensive Dictionary of Psychological and Psychoanalytical Terms*. New York : Longmans. *12*

Eysenck, H. J. (1953) *Uses and Abuses of Psychology*. London : Penguin. *94–5*

Eysenck, H. J. (1954) *The Psychology of Politics*. London : Routledge and Kegan Paul. *96–7*

Eysenck, H. J. (1957) *Sense and Nonsense in Psychology*. Harmondsworth : Penguin. *96–7*

Eysenck, H. J. and Arnold, W. (1972) *Encyclopedia of Psychology*. London : Search Press. *13*

Fast, J. (1971) *Body Language*. London : Souvenir Press. *66*

Festinger, L. (1957) *A Theory of Cognitive Dissonance*. Evanston, Ill : Row Peterson. *99–100*

Festinger, L. (1962) Cognitive dissonance. *Scientific American*. Reprint no. 472 (October edition). *99–100*

Festinger, L., Riecken, H. W. and Schachter, S. (1956) *When Prophecy Fails*. Minnesota : University of Minnesota Press. *101–8*

Gibb, C. A. (ed.) (1969) *Leadership*. Harmondsworth: Penguin. *104*

Greenspoon, T. (1955) The reinforcing effect of two spoken sounds on the frequency of two responses. *American Journal of Psychology 68*: 409–16. *64*

Hall, E. T. (1963) A system for the notation of proxemic behaviour. *American Anthropologist 65*: 1003–26. *71*

Heussenstamm, F. K. (1971) Bumper stickers and the cops. In Swingle, P. (ed.) *Social Psychology of Everyday Life*. Harmondsworth: Penguin. *19–20*

Isen, A. M. and Levin, P. F. (1973) Effect of feeling good on helping: cookies and kindness. In Swingle, P. (ed.) *Social Psychology in Everyday Life*. Harmondsworth: Penguin. *130–1*

Kogan, N. and Wallach, M. A. (1964) Risk taking as a function of the situation, the person, and the group. In Mandler, G. (ed.) *New Directions in Psychology, III*. New York: Holt, Rinehart and Winston. *108–9*

Latané, B. and Darley, J. M. (1970) *The Unresponsive Bystander: Why Doesn't He Help?* New York: Appleton-Century-Crofts. *125–7, 129–30*

Latané, B. and Rodin, J. (1969) A lady in distress: inhibiting effects of friends and strangers on bystander intervention. *Journal of Experimental and Social Psychology 5*: 189–202. *127*

Leavitt, H. J. (1951) Some effects of certain communication patterns on group performance. *Journal of Abnormal and Social Psychology 46*: 38–50. *103–4*

Lewin, K., Lippitt, R. and White, R. K. (1939) Patterns of aggression behaviour in experimentally created 'social climates'. *Journal of Social Psychology 10*: 271–99. *107–8*

Lindgren, H. C. (1969) *An Introduction to Social Psychology*. New York: Wiley. *20*

Mallott, R. W. (1973) *Humanistic Behaviourism and Social Psychology*. Michigan: Behaviordelia Inc. *44–6*

McFarland, D. and McFarland, J. (1969) *An Introduction to the Study of Behaviour*. Oxford: Basil Blackwell. *21*

McGrath, J. E. (1970) *Social Psychology: A Brief Introduction*. (2nd edn) New York: Holt, Rinehart and Winston. *13–14, 55*

McGuire, W. J. (1972) Social psychology. In Dodwell, P. C. (ed.) *New Horizons in Psychology*, 2. Harmondsworth: Penguin. *29, 30*

Milgram, S. (1963) Behavioural study of obedience. *Journal of Abnormal and Social Psychology 67*: 371–8. *121*

Milgram, S. (1965) Some conditions of obedience and dis-obedience to authority. *Human Relations 18*: 57–76. *124*

Milgram, S. (1974) *Obedience to Authority*. London: Tavistock. *119–24, 128*

Miller, G. A. and McNeil, D. (1969) Psycholinguistics. In Lindsay, G. and Aronson, E. (eds) *The Handbook of Social Psychology, Vol. 3* (2nd edn) Reading, Mass: Addison-Wesley. *59*

Moreno, J. L. (1953) *Who Shall Survive?* (2nd edn). New York: Beacon House. *105*

Orne, M. T. (1962) On the social psychology of the psychological experiment: with particular reference to demand characteristics and their implications. *American Psychologist 17*: 776–83. *25–6*

Parry, J. (1967) *The Psychology of Human Communication*. London: University of London Press. *72–5*

Pavlov, I. P. (1927) *Conditioned Reflexes*. London: Oxford University Press. *17, 33–5*

Piliavan, I., Rodin, J. and Piliavin, J. (1969) Good Samaritanism: an underground phenomenon? *Journal of Personality and Social Psychology 13*: 289–99. *128–9*

Polhemus, T. (1973) Fashion, anti-fashion and the body image. *New Society 26*: 73–6. *67*

Poussaint, A. (1971) A negro psychiatrist explains the negro psyche. In *Confrontation*. New York: Random House. *62–3*

Robinson, W. P. (1972) *Language and Social Behaviour*. Harmondsworth: Penguin. *58, 63*

Rokeach, M. (1960) *The Open and Closed Mind: Investigations into the Nature of Belief Systems and Personality*. New York: Basic Books. *96*

Rokeach, M. (1965) The nature of attitudes. In Sills, D. L. (ed.) *International Encyclopaedia of the Social Sciences*. New York: Macmillan Co. and The Free Press. *80–1*

Rosenthal, R. (1966) *Experimenter Effects in Behavioural Research*. New York: Appleton-Century-Crofts. *26–7, 66*

Ross, A. S. C. (1973) *Don't Say It*. London: Hamilton. *61*

Schlosberg, A. (1952) The description of facial expressions in terms of two dimensions. *Journal of Experimental Psychology 44*: 229–37. *69*

Seltiz, C., Jahoda, M., Deutsch, M. and Cook, S. W. (1959) *Research Methods in Social Relations*. (2nd edn). New York: Holt, Rinehart and Winston. *25–6*

Singer, R. D. (1961) Verbal conditioning and generalization of pro-democratic responses. *Journal of Abnormal and Social Psychology 63*: 43–6. *65–6*

Skinner, B. F. (1948) *Walden Two*. New York: Macmillan. *50–2*

Skinner, B. F. (1953) *Science and Human Behaviour*. New York: Macmillan. *17, 33, 36–42, 46*

Skinner, B. F. (1966) Contingencies of reinforcement in the design of a culture. *Behavioural Science 11*: 159–66. *50*

Skinner, B. F. (1971) *Beyond Freedom and Dignity*. London: Jonathan Cape. *42, 50, 59–60*

Smith, P. B. (1971) Varieties of group experience. *New Society 17*: 483–5. *110*

Sprott, W. J. H. (1952) *Social Psychology*. London: Methuen. *12–13*

Swingle, P. (1973) *Social Psychology in Everyday Life*. Harmondsworth: Penguin. *18–19, 25, 28–9*

Vygotsky, L. S. (1962) *Thought and Language*. Cambridge, Mass.: M.I.T. Press and New York: Wiley. *54–5*

Williams, C. D. (1959) The elimination of tantrum behaviour by extinction procedures. *Journal of Abnormal and Social Psychology 59*: 269–70. *42–3*

Wilson, G. D. and Patterson, J. R. (1968) A new measure of conservatism. *British Journal of Social and Clinical Psychology 7*: 264–90. *97–8*

Wheeler, L. (1966) Toward a theory of behavioural contagion. *Psychological Review 75*: 179–92. *117–19*

Wheldall, K. (1974) Social factors affecting the comprehension of pre-school children. Paper presented to the Education Section of the British Psychological Society, Edinburgh, September, 1974. *59*

Whorf, B. L. (1956) *Language, Thought and Reality*. Cambridge, Mass.: M.I.T. Press. *53*

Zajonc, R. B. (1966) *Social Psychology: An Experimental Approach*. Belmont: Wadsworth. *14, 112, 116–17*

Subject Index

142